A Woman's Guide
to the Sailing Lifestyle

The Essentials and Fun of Sailing Off the New England Coast

Debra Picchi
Thomas Desrosiers

authorHOUSE®

AuthorHouse™
1663 Liberty Drive
Bloomington, IN 47403
www.authorhouse.com
Phone: 1 (800) 839-8640

Published by AuthorHouse   09/16/2015

ISBN: 978-1-5049-2844-1 (sc)
ISBN: 978-1-5049-3372-8 (hc)
ISBN: 978-1-5049-2843-4 (e)

Library of Congress Control Number: 2015914531

Print information available on the last page.

Dedication

"This greatest of adventures of my life...
it has a name....its name is Tom."

Michael John LaChiusa, Lyrics from the score of "Tom,"

From the Musical *"Hello Again."*

This book is dedicated to my husband, Tom Desrosiers,
who made my sailing experiences possible.

Acknowledgement

We would like to acknowledge the kind support and encouragement we received from our dear friend, Anne Burke.

Table of Contents

Side Bar List

Figures

Photos and Captions

Chapter One

An Introduction:
Two Sailing Episodes

The Beginning

One spring day a friend from work named Tom invited me to go sailing. It was a sunny, warm Saturday when I drove from Keene in southwestern New Hampshire to a marina on Great Bay and the Piscataqua River in the eastern part of the state. I was in high spirits. I had never been sailing before and knew absolutely nothing about boats. But I was ready for an adventure.

I found Tom polishing what seemed to me to be a large sailboat. It was named *Trull II*, and he told me it was a 25-foot Cape Dory which I later discovered was a kind of a boat, much like a Ford is a kind of a car. I lent a hand with the cleaning until it was time for us to go out into the river. At that point I learned that we were going to take the boat down the Piscataqua River to Portsmouth Harbor and then into a small inlet named Pepperrell Cove where Tom had a permanent place for the boat. I cheerfully readied myself for the trip, grabbing my light jacket and a few other things from my car.

Tom started an outboard engine that sat in a well at the back of the boat and cast off the ropes that bound *Trull II* to the docks. He steered by moving a tiller which looked like a stick located in the center of the cockpit. We went into the river where there was a strong current that made the water churn and froth. (I later learned that the Piscataqua River is the third fastest navigable river in the world.) We struck out toward green and red cans that stood in the middle of a curve in the river in front of a large bridge. Tom explained that we had to go between the two cans because that was where the channel lay. The green can should be on our right side, the starboard side, and the red one should be on our left side, the port side. I silently tried to absorb as much information as I could and not to seem the novice I was.

Trull II chugged along valiantly through the turbulent waters. We passed between the cans toward the tall Memorial Bridge which soared above us when we went under it. I was having a wonderful time. The breeze was fresh, the water was a grey-blue, and the wooded shores revealed secluded homes every once in a while. Tom and I chatted about his boat and his personal sailing history. I learned that he had first sailed in New Orleans when he was in graduate school. He fell in love with the sport immediately and since then he had experimented with increasingly large boats until he purchased *Trull II.*

All of a sudden the engine sputtered and stopped. Tom turned to it quickly and tried to restart it, but he failed. The boat began to slide with the current toward the side of the river. I was so ignorant that I did not realize we were in a dangerous situation. Also Tom disguised his concern quite well, so I just sat there saying nothing, not wanting to distract him from dealing with the engine.

Then the boat crashed against something hard, and I was thrown on the floor of the cockpit. I quickly clambered to my feet and regained my seat as Tom cursed and said we were on the rocks. It certainly sounded like we were bumping against something. I peered over the side of the boat but could see nothing. I asked in a concerned way if they would damage the boat. Tom did not answer as he grabbed his radio and called, "May-day."

At this I became somewhat alarmed because may-day calls in the movies usually signaled something like the *Titanic* going down. I began to look around for a life preserver because I could not swim. Tom silently went down into the small cramped cabin and checked beneath the floor boards. He announced that we weren't taking on water and seemed to be relieved, so I relaxed somewhat.

Off in the distance I saw what I thought was a cute, little, red tugboat coming toward us. Its powerful engine moved it along rapidly and before too long its captain pulled it along side of us. Tom and he exchanged information and then secured *Trull II* to the tug's side after sandwiching rubber fenders between the two boats. However, the current was too strong, and it pushed the tugboat onto the rocks. Soon our two linked boats were bouncing up and down on the rocks with their captains cursing in unison.

The tugboat captain, who had his long blond hair pulled back in a pony tail, got on the radio and sent out another may-day. While we waited, Tom broke out a bottle of wine, filled plastic cups, and passed them around. The tug captain asked why I was so quiet and if I were afraid. In all truthfulness I answered that I was not. I was just trying to stay out of the way.

A powerboat appeared. The tug and powerboat captains conferred. Then a complicated maneuver took place. I found it hard to follow, but it resulted in springing both the tug and the sailboat free. The tugboat proceeded to lead us back to the marina where Tom tied the boat back on the dock. I finished my wine while Tom made arrangements to have the boat pulled out of the water and examined for damage. The boat was made of fiberglass, and the men figured that the rocks had taken gouges of glass out of the bottom of the boat. They did not believe the rocks had pierced the boat because *Trull II* still was not taking on water, which was a good sign. The manager of the marina studied the problem for a while, and then said he could get the boat back in the water within a few weeks.

Tom's face fell, and I could tell he was disappointed. He obviously really loved his boat and being on the water, and he saw this as a major setback. I was disappointed, too, because, although somewhat harrowing, my brief few hours on board the sailboat had been wonderful. I cannot say I absolutely fell in love with boating, as Tom had back when he was in his twenties. But I can say I was intrigued, perhaps as much by the beautiful river and the forests along its banks as by boating. Certainly being on the river gave me a fresh perspective of the attractions of the New Hampshire-Maine area.

However, as I thought back over the afternoon, what struck me most was the tugboat captain and Tom's expertise. They communicated with an entirely new and foreign vocabulary, and they used technology and a skill set I knew nothing about. I was not intimidated by the newness; rather, it fascinated me. I wondered if it would be possible for someone like me to learn to sail. Could I do this?

For what was left of the afternoon, Tom and I sat on board and talked about his involvement in sailing and where it had taken him. I was surprised to learn that he had sailed across the Atlantic several times in boats that were not that much larger than *Trull II.* I said that seemed extraordinary to me. He asked me why, and I tried to put my thoughts into words. Being out in the huge ocean on a relatively tiny vessel required more faith in boats and in my abilities than I had. But Tom explained that, as in most operations, the secret to success in sailing lay in back-up systems. It was imperative that for every important system on board – the sails, steering, engine -- there be a replacement. We talked more about this until the conversation easily turned to where to eat dinner.

Over the next 25 years, I revisited, time and time again, my statement about the extraordinary nature of sailing until in the end I came to understand that Tom's answer was not a complete one; rather it addressed only the technical aspect of sailing. Certainly if the engine breaks down, you need to have parts to fix it. But there is something more important than that. One needs confidence in one's self. Being able to manage fears and anxieties in the face of stormy seas and rocky shorelines is critical. Yes, it involves being able to solve problems, but even more important, it requires being able to do this by yourself. There are times when no one else is around; there is no one to ask, or to turn to for reassurance. There is fear, and there is uncertainty, but one has to keep going. This ability to persevere in spite of anxiety is vital. (That, and I guess, turning pain into fun....)

That night we drove into the town of Portsmouth. We walked around window shopping and enjoying being outdoors in the warm spring air.

Finally we decided on a restaurant and sat outside overlooking the port. Tom pointed out the huge tugboats that guided monster tankers from all over the world through Portsmouth Harbor, up the river and into the port of Portsmouth. Our marina tugboat from the afternoon looked tiny compared to those Leviathans.

Photo 1:1 Tanker Off of Portsmouth
A tanker on the Piscataqua River near the port
of Portsmouth, New Hampshire.

I didn't know then how much that day foreshadowed what was to come. The lovely river, the exciting crisis, the relaxing moments afterwards, and the exploration of foreign ports have made up a dearly-loved routine over the past twenty-five years. Tom and I married, and we have experienced this scenario so often that I truly cannot count all of our adventures. It is all part of how we have come to define The Sailing Lifestyle.

More Recently

Let's fast-forward to what happened during a recent sailing season. It was a hot summer morning when we took off on *Makai,* a thirty-seven foot Endeavour, for Stage Harbor, a wonderfully secluded cove on the north side of Cape Porpoise in southwest Maine. In the afternoon, if hot enough, we might jump off the back of the boat, and in the evening we usually sit out and watch blue herons fishing at the edge of the water. Sometimes we are alone there, but, at the most, one or two other boats join us. We thought we would spend a couple of nights anchored in this idyllic spot.

We headed out at about 9 am. The sky was overcast, and the winds were warm and gusty. A front was coming through, and the winds were out of the southwest on our stern (the back of the boat). Five-foot swells built up and pushed us along. It was easy to set our course for Stage Island Harbor once we were outside Portsmouth Harbor. Since the wind was behind us, we planned to allow the genoa (the large headsail attached to the front of the boat) to loosely billow out and pull us along. We would then set the mainsail at an angle on the other side of the boat. The idea was to let the wind fill both sails so that we would surf on top of the waves as they pushed us along. This is called sailing "wing and wing."

Photo 1:2 *Makai* Sailing "Wing and Wing"
Makai underway, sailing "Wing n Wing."

We tried this but the ride was too rough, and I was soon seasick. So we moved closer to the coast, jibing (turning the stern of the boat through the wind) and alternating between about 90 degrees east and due north. I am always uneasy when we jibe. The power of the wind as it throws the heavy mainsail from one side of the boat to the other makes a thud that I feel viscerally.

We were now traveling at a tremendous speed, clocking between six and eight knots an hour, which is of course nothing for a powerboat, but quite fast for a sailboat where you actually feel the speed more keenly. The seas hissed as we cut through them. I have read sailing books such as *Moby Dick* where Melville writes about the "oily seas." I now know what he meant. The waves were shiny black and viscous like petroleum, and they undulated as they moved under us. I sensed they were alive. It was not altogether pleasant.

The warm winds turned rainy and cool, and we put on rain gear. Tom and I took turns at the wheel, one half hour on and one half hour cuddled up in the shelter of the dodger (a canvas drape that shields the cockpit from the wind and rains). Up the coast we jibed, coming in close to look at Nubble Light off of Cape Nedick, then moving out away from land as we passed by Bald Head Cliff and the long, white strip of Ogunquit's dunes and beaches.

At about 1 pm while I was at the wheel, Tom warmed up some chicken soup, and I gratefully drank it from a mug as I watched our course. Once past Wells and Kennebunk Beaches we jibed again. By three o'clock, we were searching the coast for the opening into Stage Island Harbor. I remained at the wheel, having developed over the years an aptitude for steering *Makai* safely through lobster-pot fields. And, if you ever needed to avoid lobster pots in those days, it was in Stage Harbor. Cape Porpoise boasted of a thriving lobster industry, and the lobster men packed the entrance of the harbor with their pots topped with colorful markers. Festive but dangerous, lobster-pot ropes wrap themselves around the propeller (metal device that propels the boat through the water), shutting down the engine and holding the boat hostage. Sailors struggle to find a way to cut the rope off the prop which is underwater. To say this is not easy, especially in rough waters, is quite an understatement.

Before entering the harbor, Tom and I pulled in the genoa, took down the mainsail, and turned on the engine. Stage Harbor's narrow entrance is treacherous. The lobster pots along with fingers of rock jutting into the channel challenge sailors. We cautiously entered under power, noticing there was a sailboat nearby that looked like no one was on board. I carefully steered the boat toward the east side where we usually anchor off of a lovely beach sprinkled with boulders. Tom dropped the anchor and watched the boat carefully as it fell back. The wind had come up, and I could tell he was uneasy about the way *Makai* was moving. It is a heavy boat, and if the wind caught us, it could drag the anchor, and we would end up somewhere we did not want to be, perhaps even on the rocky island.

SIDE BAR 1:1 ANCHORING

Cruising isn't only about sailing; it is also about exploring hidden coves and islands that you wouldn't be able to access by car. Thus, you will regularly need to anchor your boat when visiting such places for swimming, lunch, sightseeing or spending the night. Select anchorages from your charts at the same time that you plan your cruise. These areas are identified with anchor symbols designating appropriate anchorages. It is important to use designated anchorages because unlisted places may be privately owned; protected areas for flora and fauna; unsuitable for anchoring due to bottom conditions, currents, hazards; or, as we once encountered, seaplane landing rights.

Figure SB 1:1 Stage Harbor Anchorage   Photo 1:1:1 Stage Harbor Entrance

Scenic Stage Harbor is beautiful, but its entrance is
treacherously filled with lobster pots.

Once you select your anchorage, study it to find the most open areas with reasonable depths. The depths on the charts are low-water depths. In Maine where tides can vary 10-12 feet, don't anchor in 5 ft. at high tide because you might end up sitting on the mud or, worse, on rocks at low tide. Also, if you anchor at high tide, remember that at low tide, the boat will tend to fall back from where you originally anchored. Estimate where your boat will be under those conditions. Hopefully you'll not be on shore. Use your depth sounder to check the depth at the chosen location. For example, if the depth is 13 feet, and you are between tides, then you may lose up to 6 feet, leaving 7 feet at low tide, which would be acceptable. Also be careful to locate all the obstacles around your anchored boat that might damage it, such as rocks, docks, lobster pots, and other boats. Factor in swing room too. A boat on anchor points into the wind, and if the wind changes, then the position of the boat will change with it. Make sure the swing room is adequate by considering the anchor and its scope.

If your boat is larger than 28 feet, you may wish to install a bow roller for your anchor. This device extends from the bow of the boat and allows the anchor rope to smoothly pay out and roll in. It also serves as a storage place for plow and Bruce anchors. And it ensures that the anchor will be instantly available in an emergency. For example, when we lost power off of Moose Island in Maine, Tom rushed to the bow and dropped the anchor within seconds of when the transmission failed. If he had had to fish the anchor out of an anchor locker, who knows what would have happened.

The next few steps in the anchoring process are to drop your anchor, let out about 25 feet of rope, reverse the boat, and snug the rope under the cleat on the bow to set the anchor. When determining how much total rope to let out once the anchor is set, experts give different advice, but most agree the more scope, the better. The scope is the ratio of the length of rode (the length of rope or chain between the anchor and the boat) let out to the depth of water. Some experts suggest between five and eight feet to one foot if you are using rope and three and five feet to one foot if you are using chain. By eight to one, I mean let out eight feet of rope for every foot of water depth at high tide. This means you have to estimate high tide depths from the low tide depths on the chart. The American Sailing Association suggests that you calculate scope using the sum of the height of the bow above the water plus the depth of water where the anchor lies multiplied by seven (ASA 2010, 103).

At various times Tom and I tried to attach markers to the anchor rope so that we could see how much rope we were letting out. We were not very successful, so in the end, we estimated the amount of rope let out by counting lengths as they passed through our hands. We did this before we dropped anchor, pulling from the anchor locker approximately how much rope we would use, leaving it neatly coiled on the bow. Avoid taking a clump of rope from the anchor locker at the last minute and throwing it overboard with the anchor, as I saw one sailor do. Needless to say, the anchor will not grab.

When you drop the anchor overboard, stand clear of the rope as it plays out. Anchors are heavy, and the rope will go overboard fast. If it catches an ankle or a hand, it can cause a sprain or a rope burn. When the boat comes to a stop, thread the anchor rope through one of the hawse holes on the port or starboard side of the bow. Do not maintain your anchorage through the bow roller. It is not sufficiently strong for the task.

Once the anchor is set, Tom always likes to take some time on deck to watch and see if everything is all right. The anchor could drag, another boat might come into the anchorage area, or an unexpected obstacle might appear. Resetting the anchor might be necessary. Be especially careful not to cross another boat's anchor line. If you are infringing on another boater's space, pull up the anchor and relocate.

If you are planning to spend the night at the anchorage or plan to leave the boat unattended for a period of time, consider increasing the length of the anchor rope and/or setting a second anchor. Tom's preferred way to set a second anchor is from the bow of the boat at an angle of approximately 45 degrees to the main anchor.

The three main anchors sailors consider having are the Bruce, the Danforth, and the Plow. The main anchor on *Makai* is a large Bruce (claw) anchor. Our second anchor is a medium-sized Fortress (Danforth style) anchor. Both of these anchors have very good holding power in sand and mud. The Fortress is made of aluminum and is quite light. This makes it ideal as the second anchor whether you set it from the pulpit or from your dingy.

The ground tackle is the anchor with its rode (the rope and/or chain between the anchor and the boat). Chain, of course, is quite heavy and holds a boat steady; however, it is hard to raise and lower by hand. *Northstar* and *Makai* had rodes made of a combination of chain and rope, but mostly of rope. I was able to release and raise *Northstar's* anchor by hand. *Makai's* anchor is heavier though, and we installed a windlass (winch used to raise the anchor) to better manage it. This winch has ended up being quite handy for a number of reasons.

I sat in the cockpit watching, and soon it was clear that the anchor was dragging. *Makai* was sliding across the harbor, caught by the wind, directly toward the other anchored boat. Tom quickly tried to get the anchor up but we were getting too close to the other boat. I turned the engine on again, while Tom ran to the back of the boat and held the other boat off, trying to protect both vessels from a damaging collision. I put the engine in gear and went forward. Tom moved rapidly to the front of the boat and continued to try to pull up the anchor. As he did so, I noticed that *Makai's* stern was coming perilously close to a lobster pot. As I struggled with avoiding the pot and steering the boat so that we could raise the anchor and reset it, we nearly fell onto the rocks. Somehow the dragging anchor had gotten wedged in a spot quite close to huge, seaweed-covered boulders that jutted out of the water.

We were in a tight spot, and none of my choices looked good to me. I called to Tom for guidance, but he could not hear me above the wind as he struggled, unaware of our predicament, on the bow of the boat with the anchor ropes. What was I to do? Drive over the lobster pot, entangling the boat and freezing the engine which would leave us without power? If we lost power, then we were totally at the mercy of the currents in the harbor. Or should I let the boat drift on the rocks hoping that they would not do that much damage? In the end I opted for the known evil. I had been on the rocks only once with *Trull II*, and the boat could have been severely damaged. But we had survived picking up many lobster pots and had managed to cope. So I opened the throttle and drove at full speed over the lobster pot and away from the rocks. I hoped that any speed we gathered before the lobster-pot ropes snared us would push the boat even further away from the rocks.

The tell-tale sound of the stalled engine let me know that we had picked up the pot, as I had predicted. I turned off the motor as Tom raised his head quizzically. He asked what happened, and I answered succinctly that we had picked up a pot. My tone might have been clipped. I went forward to help him with the anchor which we dropped again. We were not in our favorite spot in the harbor, but at this point we did not care. We just wanted the boat safely anchored away from rocks, the other sailboat, and more pots.

Back in the cockpit we had started to sit down to figure out what to do when Tom leapt up again. The anchor was dragging once more. This was unbelievably bad luck. And now, of course, we had no engine to help us control the boat. We were at the mercy of the wind as we started to slide across the harbor. Tom, who thinks very fast, yelled at me to help him get the dinghy engine in place. He would take a second anchor he had stored in a locker, called a Fortress anchor, into the dinghy and drop it away from the boat to stop it from sliding. Moving as fast as I could, I detached the dinghy engine from its stand and handed it down to him from *Makai's* stern. He attached it to dinghy. Then he drove to the bow of *Makai*, where I raced, handing him the Fortress anchor and untangling the rope that held it to the boat. He quickly drove the dingy in the opposite direction from the neighboring boat and well away from the rocky coast where he dropped the anchor. I fed out a lot of rope. Then I wrapped it around an engine-driven winch (motor) on the bow of the boat that we use for pulling up the anchor. As the winch spun, I slowly pulled on the rope, moving *Makai,* inch by inch, away from the dangers. Tom inspected the situation from the dinghy, and then returned to climb up the ladder to the cockpit.

Now we had two anchors out in a stirrup fashion. We both believed the second anchor was doing most of the work, but we left the first one in place just in case. Exhausted and demoralized we sat in the cockpit looking at each other. We had never had such a bad day. Dragging anchors, rocks, lobster pots, nearly crashing into other boats. It was so bad, it was almost comical.

After we rested a bit, Tom donned a wet suit, took a sharp knife, and went overboard into the icy Maine waters in an effort to go under the boat and cut the pot line off the propeller. But the winds and current bounced him off the side of the boat, and, eventually, defeated, he dejectedly came back on board.

I took care over dinner that night, feeling that we needed cheering up after our traumatic day. Not only did I not want us to dwell on what had happened, which would spoil our weekend, but I wanted our attention to shift to the extraordinary beauty that surrounded us. As I cooked, I looked out of the galley (kitchen) porthole (window). The sun was setting over the trees, and orange ribbons of light danced in the water. The line of the trees met the granite rocks in a quintessentially-Maine way. We ate in the cockpit and lingered over glasses of red wine as evening set in. The cry of the herring gulls punctuated the rhythm of the waves crashing on the beach.

The sky and water slowly melted together into a grey-blue. The tide was out, and the black rocks stood out against the store. Suddenly I heard the tell-tale squawks of the great blue heron. I turned to see three of these amazing birds flying low in the sky. Their legs were held back against their bodies as they glided into the harbor from the east. With exquisite daintiness they dropped their gangly legs down and majestically landed on the rocks in front of us. There they stayed during the night before moving on in the morning. I remember thinking that it was moments like these that made all the problems we'd had that day worth it.

SIDE BAR 1:2 HERONS AND LOONS

One of the unexpected joys of sailing, and especially of being on anchor where you can relax with a pair of binoculars, is watching birds. We have several field guides in our on-board library that we discovered in used bookstores while on cruise, including wonderful, old copies of The Audubon Society Field Guide to North American Birds – Eastern Region by John Bull and John Farrand, Jr. (1977) and Peterson Field Guides - Eastern Birds by Roger Tory Peterson (1980). Newer guides we use are Peterson Field Guide to Birds of North America by Roger Tory Person (2008) and Smithsonian Nature Guide - Birds by David Burnie (2012). One piece of understanding we have gleaned from using books published at different times is how dynamic the fluctuations of the bird populations are. Dramatic changes have taken place in the relatively short time I have been sailing.

Having established our sources, I want to add a disclaimer. Neither Tom nor I are ornithologists, but hopefully we haven't made too many mistakes in our identification efforts. Below and in subsequent side bars I describe some birds we frequently see while under sail or while on anchor. The list is not comprehensive; rather, it includes a couple of our favorites.

Tom and I rarely see loons in Pepperrell Cove, and I remember the first time I saw one there with its distinctive checkered back and white and black collar. We were on our mooring, and I was staring idly at a bird that I saw swimming in the cove. All of a sudden, I sat up straight in amazement and called Tom. It was a loon, black and white with the dagger-like bill it's famous for. Peterson describes its cry as "falsetto wails, weird yodeling, maniacal quavering laughter" (1980, p. 32). I didn't hear its call that night unfortunately. I suspect it would have been memorable.

A bird I always associate with Stage Harbor, Maine is the great blue heron where we saw five and six at a time, fishing on the shore. These gorgeous, large, fishing birds can grow to 4 feet. They have lovely blue-grey feathers and yellow bills. They fly

---

with their necks folded and their legs positioned in a characteristic fashion, so that it is hard to miss them in the air. They have hoarse, guttural squawks. One night Tom and I were anchored in Gosport Harbor off of Star Island in the Isles of Shoals. The Isles tend to be a bit noisy because of all of the seagulls, but all of a sudden a very foreign-sounding squawk came from the top of *Makai's* mast. It was already dark with no moon so at first we could not see what was up there. Tom went down under to get a large flashlight which we trained upwards. There, flapping about in distress, was a great blue heron. We tried to make it leave because we were afraid it would damage the equipment that is attached to the top of the mast. But it just flapped around up there all night. I figured it did not want to move to one of the islands because of the gulls. Probably our mast provided a temporary safe haven for it. The next morning it was gone. In New Hampshire we tend to see them more in marshes and swamps; however, we sometimes spot them on the coast.

The green heron is another interesting bird we've seen. One memorable night in Riggs Cove off of Robinhood Cove in Maine, we were sitting out in the cockpit watching dusk gather and the light fade. In front of us on the shore appeared a green heron with its green-blue back and chestnut neck. It daintily strutted about in the water as it fished before disappearing into the dark. The field guides state that these herons are common, but we rarely see them (compared to the great blue herons), perhaps because they tend to be retiring, according to the Audubon guide (Bull and Farrand 1977, 444).

The next day Tom tried again to cut us loose from the lobster pot again, but the winds and seas were still too heavy. We spent the day on the beach gathering mussels from under the seaweed to steam that night. We splashed around in the cold water and took a long walk on the beach. That night, after dinner, we sat out again and watched the gathering dusk as we listened to a jazz CD.

The third morning, Tom hose-clamped a formidable-looking serrated knife to a telescoping-pick-up pole and determinedly climbed into the dingy. I went with him. War had been declared. As I held the little boat steady, he attacked the rope wrapped around the propeller with all his strength. In a surprisingly short time, he was able to cut the tangle of lobster-pot ropes from around the prop. And we were free. It had just taken the right tool.

SIDE BAR 1:3 LOBSTER POTS

Tom will bend the ear of anyone who will listen to him about the dangers of lobster pots. And as one who has experienced getting caught in them right by his side, I agree with him. We both enjoy a good boiled lobster or two better than most people. Yet, it has been tempting, from time to time, to boycott this delicacy as a way to send a message to the lobstermen who set their traps in some of the most beautiful anchorages and passages of Maine. These traps sit and wait to snare your propeller or rudder or any other piece of equipment that gets near them.

As you can see from the diagram, the pots are attached to a large buoy which generally floats vertically in the water. These are painted bright colors so that the lobsterman can find his pots. This helps us see them and avoid them as well. However, the lobstermen have taken to attaching a line from the buoy to a small piece of cork. This is done, presumably, to enable them to wrap the line around their winch and raise the pot. The downside, unfortunately, is that this line floats horizontally from the buoy to the toggle and can get caught in the boat's propeller, stalling the engine.

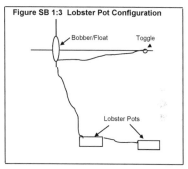

Figure SB 1:3 Lobster Pot Configuration

Trull II had an outboard, and we had little trouble with pots. I believe that this was before the toggle system was introduced. *Northstar* had the propeller protected by the keel and rudder and escaped getting caught by traps. However, *Makai* picked up pots regularly, causing us great inconvenience. It was after we nearly went on the rocks in Townsend Gut between Ebenecook and Boothbay that Tom resolved to solve the problem.

Townsend Gut is a narrow passage with a swing bridge at mid point. It has strong currents, so you have to approach the bridge carefully and maintain position until it opens. There seem to be a million pots in Townsend Gut, and why this is permitted I cannot understand. We were in line for the bridge when the motor stalled. It was a pot. Fortunately, it shook off, and we were able to restart the engine, avoiding disaster.

Tom, a born problem solver, began to think about solutions. We needed a device to prevent the line from approaching the propeller. The Endeavour 37 has a free standing rudder not connected to the keel at the bottom. In his own words, "I contacted a New Hampshire company that sells marine-grade stainless steel and bought 2 pieces of ¼-inch thick 2-inches x 2-inches angle-steel. I ran them from two feet before the end of the keel out beyond the rudder with flat sides down. I secured them to the keel with 6 stainless steel bolts 3/8 inches in diameter. I then bought 2 pieces of ¼-inch stainless steel 3 inches wide. I ran these from the hull above and before the rudder to the angle pieces below. These were also secured in both locations with 3/8-inch stainless steel bolts. Everything was very heavily caulked prior to assembly. I can report that the arrangement worked very well. We still picked up the occasional toggle and rope but, by and large, our boat was pot free. And, I can still enjoy my lobsters!"

Tom built a metal preventer to protect *Makai's* propeller from lobster pots.

If this seems a bit complicated and intimidating, don't worry. It did to me too. To ease into the sailing lifestyle, you don't have to know all of the facts right away. But it pays to know about some of the problems

Photo SB 1:3:1 Lobster Pot Preventer

and to understand that someone out there can probably solve them for you.

We spent one more night in Stage Harbor. The boat had turned in the wind so the cockpit now faced the rocky opening of the cove. As the surf splashed against the rocks, glittering spray dashed up into the air and lit up the night. It must have been the phosphorus in the water to make such a spectacular show. Then the moon rose, a cold, silver luminous orb in the sky.

The next morning we pulled up the first anchor and discovered, as we suspected, that it had not bitten into the mud. Tom muttered that next year he would replace it with a heavier anchor, maybe even a Bruce anchor, which was known for its clawed configuration and tremendous holding power. Using the winch we pulled up the second anchor which clearly had been holding us. It was set deep in the mud and took some manipulating to pull it free. Then I took the wheel, and *Makai* serenely moved through the lobster pots that lay on the water like colored beads and on out into the ocean, heading for home.

Twenty-five years of sailing lie between the two episodes described in this chapter. I still cannot swim (that well) or fix an engine, but in addition to handling the boat under power and moving through lobster-pot fields, I know how to plan a passage using maps and charts to determine a course, set a course and navigate with the help of GPS equipment (Global Position System), talk on a two-way radio, trim sails (set sails in a variety of positions), jibe and tack, throw out an anchor, pick up a mooring pick-up pole or slimy mooring rope in the water, and help bring a boat alongside a dock when the wind is making everything twice as hard.

The knowledge and experience I now possess have been hard-won over the years. I frequently say to my husband with some irony that during my first sailing experiences I felt little or no anxiety in spite of some difficult moments. But now, so many years later, I have learned fear. Sometimes this is a good thing because fear teaches you to avoid mistakes. But sometimes, there are moments when I yearn for the comfort of ignorance. In this book I describe how I learned what I know. And I offer my knowledge, little that it is, to those who may be interested in The Sailing Lifestyle.

I mention "women" in the title of this book because, for whatever historical and cultural reasons, more men are involved in sailing than women. In many of the yacht clubs that we have visited or belonged to, you find single men involved but rarely a single woman on her own. And in Pepperrell Cove I have seen only two sailboats owned by a woman; the rest are owned by men or man/woman couples. In this book, I hope to encourage especially women (but men, of course, too) to seriously consider getting involved in this rich and rewarding world. In the final chapter of this book, I discuss resources available for women who are interested.

Yet, this memoir is not just about the essentials of sailing. It is more encompassing than that because The Sailing Lifestyle is about more than knowing how to make a sailboat go. It is about allowing the sailboat to take you to places you've never been and would probably never go if not for sailing. It is about experiencing these places differently than you would if you were traveling in another way. It's about slowing down and seeing the world differently – savoring and relishing it. Thus, in this book, I talk about small coastal New England communities we discovered and how much we enjoyed wandering around in them and talking to people we met there. So it is part travel literature too, and I would not want that to be minimized or totally eclipsed by the sailing dimension.

The Sailing Lifestyle is also about being in close contact with other people for long periods of time during which you intensely work and live together. You face crises and see where you and your fellow sailors are weak and where you are strong. You learn to cooperate and compensate when others are sick and can't function or when they have their heads in the engine locker for hours while you handle the wheel and the sails when you were really looking forward to a hot meal and a bunk. But neither of you have any other choice. That's just the way it is for that moment, that hour. And you accept what you have to do with as much grace and humor as you can pull off.

A final suggestion is that as you read through the text, go online and call up satellite maps of the coast of New England. Have these in front of you as you read because it is helpful to visually follow along as I discuss sailing off the coast of New Hampshire, Massachusetts, and Maine. As an aid, in each chapter I refer to specific map coordinates for you to study. This is not a bad exercise in-and-of-itself because it will familiarize you with maps and the concepts of longitude and latitude and how they change as a boat moves through space.

Chapter Two

Getting to Know the Boat

Each boat is different. And yet once I was familiar with one boat, it was easy to get used to other boats. In this chapter I describe *Makai* (a 37-foot Endeavour) and make references to *Northstar* (a 28-foot Pearson Triton), and *Trull II* (a 25-foot Cape Dory), the first boat on which I seriously sailed. I would like to suggest that new sailors scan through this chapter and return to it from time to time as they need specific information because the level of detail and new vocabulary words might seem daunting at first glance. If you are put off at first, let me assure you that if I managed to pick up this information over time, then so can anyone. Also, I define a term the first time I use it, and after that, I assume the reader will remember the definition. A glossary at the end of the book provides basic information, should your memory need refreshing.

SIDE BAR 2:1 TYPES OF SAILBOATS

Some differentiate types of sailing boats on the basis of size of boat, its function, and the presence or absence of a keel which is a heavy structure made of lead or iron that is part of the hull of a boat. It keeps the boat upright and provides stability when under sail (Sleight 2001, 37- 41, 58).

Our first dinghy was not an inflatable one. It was made of fiberglass. Gulls loved to sit in it, hoping for treats.

Photo SB 2:1:1 Dinghy and Sea Gull

Using these criteria, the smallest sailboat is a dinghy which is about 10 to 12 feet long. It lacks a keel; rather it has centerboard or a daggerboard that retracts into a compartment in the hull. Stability is provided by the body weight of the sailor(s) which can shift as needed. Dinghies are used in learning how to sail because they are very responsive, and the consequences of each sailing decision are quite obvious. They are also used in racing, and in any number of harbors into which Tom and I sailed or motored, we had to pick our way carefully through dinghies that seemed to fly through the water around us.

A second kind of sailing boat described by some boaters is a keelboat that is about 20 to 30 feet long and that has either a full keel or a smaller fin keel. These sailboats are less responsive than dinghies because of their size, but they are drier and more comfortable. Technically, by this definition, *Trull II* and *Northstar* were keelboats since the Cape Dory was 25 feet, and the Triton was 28 feet. Keelboats are good for learning how to sail as well as for overnight trips. Tom and I traveled in *Northstar* to York, Maine and the Isles of Shoals where we frequently spent the night.

Cruisers are a third type of sailing boat. They are 30 feet long or more and are particularly good for cruising. There is plenty of room on board for the crew to move around, prepare food, and sleep. Although some believe they are too large for learning to sail, I did indeed learn quite a bit about sailing on these larger sailboats. One can also learn to navigate on them, to understand the weather and its effects on sailing, and to practice moving sails about under specific conditions.

So that is one classification system. I have developed my own personal system though, and I would encourage you to also. I learned to classify sailboats by watching them under way on the water or on moorings and anchorages. Two types of boats I recognize but don't deal with a lot are those that I see as being too small - dinghies and widgeons for example – and those that I see as being too large – schooners and clippers for example. Tom and I of course rely on a dinghy to travel to and from *Makai* for instance, but we don't sail it. Widgeons are somewhat larger, 12 feet or so in length, and they are considered true sailboats, rather than dinghies with sails on them. Schooners are considerably larger with two to six masts. In the past they were used for shipping and fishing. Clippers typically had three masts with large square sails and were famous for their great speed, traveling hundreds of miles in a single day. This made them very popular with the nineteenth-century shipping industry.

A third type of sailboat is a multi-hulled boat such as a catamaran. These boats are reportedly lighter and faster than mono-hulled boats, such as the ones I discuss below, and they can go into shallower water because they lack keels. We don't see many catamarans in Pepperrell Cove.

The most important types of boat in my personal classification system are the sloop, ketch, and yawl, and, of these three, the sloop is the kind of boat that I know the best. It has one mast with a mainsail and a headsail that can be a genoa, a smaller jib, and a larger, billowy spinnaker. By headsail, I mean a sail that is attached to the bow of the boat. *Makai, Northstar,* and *Trull II* are all sloops.

Photo SB 2:1:2 *Makai* on land.

Makai on land.

Ketches and yawls, frequently seen in Pepperrell Cove as well as when we cruise along the coast of Massachusetts, New Hampshire, and Maine, have two masts instead of one. In the case of the ketch, there is a main mast and a smaller mizzen mast which carries a mizzen sail. The latter is located behind the main mast but in front of the rudder. With a yawl, the mizzen mast lies behind both the main mast and the rudder. It is smaller than the ketch's mizzen sail, used more for balance than to propel the sailboat.

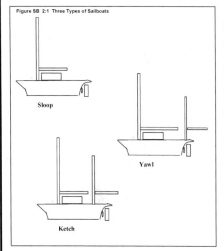

Figure SB 2:1 Three Types of Sailboats.

Sloops, ketches, and yawls vary in length. When I asked Tom with which type of boat he'd ideally like to sail off the coast of Maine, he did not hesitate, but immediately said, a yawl of about 35 to 40 feet in length. He mentioned in particular that he liked the idea of being under sail or on anchorage with the mizzen sail as a stabilizing force. And a sailboat of about 35 to 40 feet would be a good size for two people to handle. I agree with this, but I would also be comfortable with an even smaller sloop or yawl. Although a larger boat gives you more room, it requires more maintenance as well. When we switched from the 28-foot *Northstar* to the 37-foot *Makai,* I noticed a significant difference in the amount of time Tom and I spent cleaning the hull, working on the brightwork, painting the underside, and working on the interior. I guess each individual and couple must sit down and weigh the costs and benefits of each option. Then they can make the choice that suits them best.

Above Deck

The captain and his or her crew sail the boat from the deck and cockpit. The cockpit is either located in the back of the boat (an aft cockpit), as it is with *Makai,* or in the center of the boat in which case it is called the center cockpit. I once sailed in the Caribbean on a sailboat that had a center cockpit. The thing that I remember the most about it was that down under, behind the cockpit, there was a huge cabin with its own head (toilet) that slept at least two. I considered that boat quite luxurious. More experienced sailors than I would make more substantive observations and address structural issues, such as steering problems.

Whether the cockpit of centrally located or an aft cockpit, there are benches inside it covered with cushions, where the crew and passengers can sit. We also have a small table that collapses against the wheel when we are not using it. When on anchor or on a mooring, we put drinks and dishes on the table.

Photo 2:1 *Northstar's* Deck
Northstar's deck, clearly showing the cockpit, topsides, mast, and boom.

The cockpit needs to be self draining. That way, if it takes on any water, the water passes through drains and out of the boat. *Makai* is not a "wet" boat. That is, it sits high up out of the water, and waves rarely reach up to wash in. However, *Northstar* and *Trull II* were wet boats. They sat low in the water, and when we heeled (pushed over by wind on one side), water would splash up on to us and into the boat. Keeping the drains unclogged and clean is particularly important with "wet" boats.

Water-tight storage lockers lie on either side of the cockpit and at the stern. We store life preservers, fenders, ropes, mops, brooms, pick-up poles, and other boat gear in them. At the front of the cockpit is a hatch (door) that leads inside the boat. It is sealed with wooden slats when we are not there or sailing in heavy weather. A dodger (canvas shield with plastic windows that arches over the companionway) protects the hatch when it is open and provides a place out of the wind and rain for crew members.

Winches (mechanical devices for pulling in and letting out ropes or wires) for the sail sheets (ropes that position sails) and halyards (ropes that pull up and let down sails) are located within easy reach of someone kneeling or sitting in the cockpit. In front of the wheel is a binnacle (a waist-high stand) which houses the compass, one of two GPS devices, and one of two depth gauges. We navigate the boat using these instruments. I will discuss this in detail in a later chapter. The wheel, which is used for steering, is located toward the back of the cockpit. Sailboats have either tillers or wheels. *Makai* has a wheel, and *Northstar* and *Trull II* had tillers. We have had problems with both. Once while we were sailing on *Makai*, the steering cables slipped off their pulleys. Tom attached an emergency steering tiller to a socket that allowed us to steer while he got the cables back into their tracks.

We've also had trouble with *Northstar's* tiller which turned into a real adventure. We were on our way back from York Harbor, which has a difficult harbor to enter (see 70.636 degrees west longitude 43.130 north latitude). You have to navigate a "dog's leg" passageway to get up into the York River, first motoring west, then northeast, then west again. It is inadvisable to try to do this in the fog or at night, unless you have, what they call, "local knowledge." Once beyond the "dog's leg," boats are no longer allowed to anchor, so you have to call the harbormaster for a mooring.

One weekend Tom and I decided to sail up to York Harbor, stay the night, and return the next day. York Harbor lies north to northeast of Portsmouth Harbor, and the wind was gently blowing from the southwest. We had a lovely ride up the coast, running before the warm breeze. Once there, we secured a mooring and walked to the town beach which is a crescent of white sand. We also found the Cliff Walk which took us along the harbor and in back of some of the lovely homes that distinguish York. After dinner on board, we sat out and listened to music.

By the time we went to bed, however, the wind picked up, and when we got up the next morning, Tom and I were facing, not gentle breezes from the southwest, but gusty offshore winds (winds blowing from the land toward the sea). The temperature had dropped too. That meant we would be beating (sailing into the wind) back to Portsmouth Harbor, and it looked like it would be a cold, rough ride. Seas had built up by the time we made it through the "dog's leg," so as we sailed out of York Harbor, we had our hands full trying to keep *Northstar* pointed toward a spot between the Isles of Shoals and Portsmouth. Although Whaleback Lighthouse lies at the mouth of the Portsmouth Harbor, we could not steer towards it because we had to go around the East and West Sisters, nasty rocks off Garrish Island. Once that we had sailed past the big whistle called "2KR," we could be confident we'd past the worst of the rocks. Then we would we turn *Northstar* to the northwest and head directly into Portsmouth Harbor.

Depending on how you look at winds and seas, the ride was either exhilarating or terrifying. Not only did the waves buffet us, but the wind constantly pushed us off course. The strain was too much for the tiller, and it broke into two pieces with a great crack. We were left with no way to steer the boat. As the waves tossed us around, Tom, who is a resourceful problem-solver, grabbed some hose clamps and a couple of pieces of steel and splinted the upper piece of the tiller to the lower. We limped into Pepperrell Cove later that day.

So those are some of the adventures we've had with wheels and tillers. Let's get back to the boat layout. The roof of the cabin makes up the middle section of the deck. On smaller sailboats the mast sits on top of the cabin, while on *Makai* the mast passes through the cabin and into the keel (part of the hull made of heavy material that provides ballast and stability to a sailboat). On either side of the roof of the cabin, side decks allow the crew to pass from the cockpit to the foredeck in front of the mast. There are handrails to grasp on the top of the roof when on the side deck. Safety lines also prevent the crew from falling off the side of the boat. They stretch from the stern (the back of the boat) to the bow (the front of the boat). Frankly, I become very nervous when Tom passes from the cockpit to the foredeck when we are underway, and the seas are rough and the wind strong. I always want him to wear a safety line so if a wave crashes over the bow of the boat or if he loses his footing, he will not go over-board.

The foredeck contains navigational lights for traveling at night (we will discuss that later) and hawseholes (for anchoring and mooring lines). The anchor locker which stores several anchors is embedded in the foredeck. On either side of the anchor locker is a large cleat (a metal devise to which a rope can be secured). You can attach an anchor or a mooring line to this devise. One of the hardest things I had to learn when I first helped Tom anchor *Northstar* was to thread the anchor line, which is actually supporting the weight of the entire boat when the boat is on anchor, through the hawsehole and cleat it. If I left the line on a handrail rather than passing it through the hawseholes, it could tear out the handrail. And if I left it on the bow of the boat rather than cleating it off, then not only would I have lost the anchor and the anchor line, but the boat would have drifted.

On the top of the mast is a Windex, a mechanical wind vane, which shows the direction the wind is blowing and is clearly visible from the cockpit. In addition there is a wind sensor that transmits information about the wind direction and speed to a display in the cockpit. This shows the wind speed and direction which is particularly important for night sailing when the Windex is not visible. We also get readings about the wind and seas from the marine radio that we can access through our two-way radio.

SIDE BAR 2:2 BEAUFORT'S WIND SCALE

To understand wind speed, sailors depend on the Beaufort Wind Scale that was devised by the English admiral Sir Francis Beaufort in the nineteenth century. This scale categorizes wind strength and assigns numbers to each level, going from one to fifteen. Force 3 is ideal for learning to sail in a small sailboat because the boat is responsive without there being the danger of capsizing. Force 6 is very strong and should be avoided by sailors in small boats, although larger keelboats can handle greater force winds (Sleight 2001, 119).

One, on the Beaufort scale, signifies that the winds are blowing between one and three knots (nautical miles) per hour. There are ripples on the water, and smaller boats should be able to sail, but sailboats that are the size of *Makai* will need to motor in such winds because of its weight. Two on the scale is winds at four to six knots; this is considered a light breeze, and you can feel the wind on your face. Small wavelets form on the water. Motoring will still be the preferred option with a boat like *Makai*, although light racing boats may be able sail with those winds. Three is a gentle breeze with wind speeds between seven and ten knots. Large wavelets with breaking crests will be visible. Four on the scale counts as a moderate breeze of 11 to 16 knots. While these conditions are ideal for a heavy boat like *Makai*, dinghies should head for shore. Waves can reach over three feet, and there are white caps. Force Five is 17 to 21 knots, and these winds are called "fresh." There are moderate-sized waves of up to seven feet with frequent white horses (foam-crested waves). Six on the scale means that the winds have really picked up, blowing between 22 and 27 knots. These winds are "strong," and the seas are building. At six on the Beaufort scale, large waves of up to twelve feet with foamy crests and spray make sailing difficult and uncomfortable. Large trees are swaying, and it would be hard to use an umbrella. Between seven and 12 on the scale, things get progressively worse until the scale ominously reads that sailors are in danger, and "survival is the most one can hope for" (Maloney 2003, 838, Sleight 2001, 119). (Force 12 is hurricane wind. Sleight notes that the Beauford Scale goes up to Force 15, but doesn't provide details, and neither does Maloney.)

I have never been on *Makai* under severe conditions, but when Tom brought the boat to South Carolina from St. Thomas in the Caribbean, he and his crew passed through a storm. Tom said it was pretty hairy. The wind was very strong, and the waves were formidable. I was glad I was not on board.

Rigging and Sails

Descriptions of the sails and rigging (the system of wires and ropes that are used to keep the mast in place and to position the sails) can be quite technical. In this section, I describe only the basic facts. I must say that I have never felt compelled to learn the name of every possible sail and all the ropes. And I manage nonetheless.

We have established that *Makai* is a sloop. On either side of the single mast run three metal shrouds that support it. Spreaders provide support for the upper part of the mast as the main shroud runs through the end of the spreader and is attached to the mast. The other two shrouds run from the deck to a point about three quarters up the mast. The forestay supports the mast in the front of the boat and the roller-furling mechanism for the headsails, and an aft stay supports the mast from the stern of the boat. The boom is attached to the mast at a right angle. The topping lift which runs from the end of the boom to the top of the mast holds the boom up at a right angle so it does not sink onto the cabin top.

We also know that *Makai* has a mainsail and a headsail. Tom and I almost always have the mainsail up, no matter what the conditions, because it is so versatile. It can be used in both the lightest wind, to stabilize the boat, and the heaviest wind, when it can be reefed (shortened) to reduce the sail area and, indirectly, the speed of the boat. To raise the mainsail Tom goes to the middle deck where the mast is located and pulls on the halyard. Once the sail is partially hoisted, the halyard is wrapped twice around the winch; the winch handle is inserted; and the winch is cranked to raise the sail to its proper height. The halyard is then cleated with the winch taking the main pressure. (Tip: always remove the winch handle and return it to the cockpit after the sail is hoisted.)

The mainsail is attached to the mast and the boom. The boom juts over the middle and back part of the deck. (See Photo 2:1.) The angle of the mainsail is controlled by the mainsheet which is attached to the cockpit deck. To take down the mainsail, we release the mainsheets until the mainsail flaps in the wind. Then one of us pulls the boom to the center of the cockpit and secures it, while the other of us releases the halyard so the mainsail drops. On *Northstar*, I normally went forward to the mast and released the halyard. *Makai's* equipment is set too high for me to reach so Tom is the one who usually goes forward and releases it. Once released, the sail falls down, and the two of us fold it on top of the boom. Tom likes the mainsail to be tautly and neatly furled on top of the boom which involves the two of us repeatedly pulling the mainsail back toward the stern of the boat until it is tightly and smoothly bundled. Tom also prefers to leave the main halyard secured to the mainsail so he draws the halyard down under the winch and secures it with a cleat. This both prevents what remains of the sail that is exposed from being caught by the wind and stops the halyards from clanking about and keeping people in neighboring boats awake at night.

Sloops also have headsails which are attached to the forestay on the bow of the boat. The headsail we depend on the most is the genoa but other sails are the jib (small sail) and the spinnaker (large sail). Any headsail can be used in a number of ways. There are winches on the port and starboard sides of the cockpit. The headsail sheets are attached to one or the other of these winches which can be used to pull the sheet in tautly, thus pulling the genoa back, or let the sheet out loosely, thus allowing the genoa to billow out and fill with wind, all depending on the wind and course. Once the sail is set at the appropriate angle, the sheet is cleated. Taking down the headsail can be done in a number of ways depending on the boat. If the boat has roller-furling equipment, like *Makai* does, then Tom or I loosen the sheets off of the winches in the cockpit and pull on a line that rolls the sail around the forestay. *Northstar* and *Trull II* did not have roller-furling equipment, so when it was time to take in the genoa, Tom had to go onto the foredeck, pull the sail down, and stuff it into a sail bag. If there were seas and a lot of wind, I worried about him bouncing up and down on the foredeck of the boat.

Down Under: The Inside of the Boat

A friend and her parents came sailing one day with us, and I was surprised to notice that they carefully remained in the cockpit of the boat rather than going inside where I expected them to explore the galley, cabins, and head. My friend later explained they had been afraid of getting seasick so they had stayed out in the air where they could see land. I love the inside of boats and never get tired of exploring one more.

The companionway allows access from the cockpit to the main cabin below. There are bunks on either side which I think of as sofas. When the weather is fine, we tend to be up in the cockpit enjoying the views. But when it rains or is cold, we curl up on a bunk and read or listen to the radio or CDs.

Under the bunks there are drawers where Tom and I store things. Over the years I have fought hard to retain control of just two of the six drawers where I store canned and dried food supplies. Tom, like an amoeba, has spread his tools into the other four drawers, and he would have no trouble filling the food drawers too. When I accuse him of turning the boat into a floating toolbox, he reasonably points out that when you are on the water and something goes wrong, you need a wide selection of tools for fixing the problem. When on board he sees the boat as something like a self-sufficient spacecraft.

Off the main cabin there is a galley with a propane stove which is gimbaled (rings keep the stove horizontal when the boat rolls). The stove has three burners, and we do most of our cooking on them. We used to grill steaks or chicken off the back of the boat, but the seagulls defeated us. I have a vivid memory of being in the cockpit while Tom grilled some beef. Huge black-backed and herring gulls swooping down around us, seeing who could get closest to the meat. I felt like I was in Hitchcock's *The Birds*.

Makai had an electric refrigerator when we purchased it, but Tom replaced it with an ice chest which we think makes more sense. At the beginning of a ten-day cruise, we fill this chest with six ice blocks (blocks and not ice cubes which melt too rapidly), and they last the entire trip. In the chest we keep about three days' worth of chicken, beef, cream, juice, butter, and cheese. A small net hammock strung from port latches keeps our fresh vegetables and salads for us. We plan on visiting a grocery store about twice on a cruise, purchasing just a few days' worth of supplies at a time. This system has worked well for us over many years.

Makai's galley has a set of sinks and small cabinets for storing pots, dishes, and utensils. The sinks are deep so that, when under way, water does not splash out. The cabinets have strong latches on them so that once things are stowed away, they will not fall out, should the boat heel.

The main cabin is also were the all-important charts are stored and studied. When on cruise, it is imperative that each morning we chart a course for the day. At first we used only charts and a compass. Later, GPS technology embedded the National Oceanic and Atmospheric Administration (NOAA) charts in their software and gave sailors pictures of the area with the boat's position and progress clearly shown. Understanding the course and its relationship to latitude and longitude readings are critical, and we discuss these topics more in later chapters.

Photo 2:2 *Makai's* Chart Table, Oil Lamp, Foul Weather Gear
Makai's chart table is an important hub of planning and
writing logs. The oil lamp is used at night to conserve power.
Foul weather gear is stored in a locker unless it is wet.

Across from the galley is the aft cabin. Unless we have visitors, we use this cabin for storage, throwing extra sleeping bags and clothes on the bunk. There is also a little vanity and sink with a mirror, a locker where we hang jackets, and drawers for clothes, linens, and towels. Tom and his crew that brought *Makai* from the Virgin Islands took turns sleeping in the aft cabin bunk which snugly fits against the hull of the boat on one side and the wall of the cockpit on the other. You clamber in from the top of the bunk. The two main advantages of this bunk are that it is quite far back in the boat which means there is less motion, and when in it, you cannot fall out of it if the boat heels to one side. Tom reported to me that it was quite comfortable on that passage.

Beyond the main cabin lie the head and the forward cabin. For those who remember *Moby Dick* by Herman Melville and *Two Years Before the Mast* by Richard Henry Dana, this part of the boat is referred to as the forecastle or the foc'sle. It is the area in front of the mast where, in larger sailing boats than ours, the crew's quarters are located. The officers normally had their quarters aft where there is less motion. In reading *Moby Dick* I got the distinct impression that the sailors enjoyed themselves more than the officers despite being relegated to the foc'sle. They had a lot of fun playing cards and drinking their tots of rum.

Our forward cabin has a large double V-shaped birth where Tom and I usually sleep unless the weather is really bad. It has two lockers and a set of drawers for clothing. This cabin is very airy because there is a large hatch above the birth and a port on each side of the cabin. Even on the hottest summer nights, the cross-ventilation from the ports and hatch provided a cooling breeze. For extra air we added a brightly-colored stocking that attaches to the hatch and funnels air down into the cabin. We never wished for air conditioning.

The head is located off the main and forward cabins with a door to each. The head has a toilet that allows you to pump in water from outside and then flush waste into a holding tank that we have pumped out at a marina periodically. When I first started sailing with Tom, the rules were not so strict about how sailors disposed of human-waste.

But awareness has grown of the dangers of contaminating both the waters that people use as well as natural ecosystems, so we have become increasingly careful about keeping our holding tank properly functioning. And having a large, well-vented holding tank is essential for pleasurable cruising. *Makai* originally had a seventeen-gallon tank, and we upgraded to a thirty-seven-gallon tank so that we could venture into more secluded areas, such as rivers and distant coves, where there were no pump-out stations.

SIDE BAR 2:3 WASTE MANAGEMENT SYSTEMS FOR CRUISING YACHTS

A suitable waste containment system (holding tank) is required by law for all boats with sleeping accommodations. The holding tank accumulates human waste and is periodically pumped out at marinas or municipal facilities. This protects the ocean/lake waters from contamination which is harmful to humans, animals, and aquatic life using or inhabiting the body of water.

The principle of a holding tank system is simple. Water from the sea is pumped into the toilet through a seacock (a valve in an opening/hole of the boat's hull permitting water to flow into the vessel). This water with the waste from the toilet is pumped into the holding tank as the toilet is flushed. The waste remains in the tank until you decide to pump it out. This is an important point. When planning a cruise, build in stops where you can pump the tank out. These facilities have become readily available, so when you stop to buy fuel and fill up your water tank, pump out your holding tank too.

Figure SB 2:3 Legal System for Waste Management

If you have a large boat and sail with guests or like long cruises with many remote anchorages, consider installing a large (35-50) gallon holding tank. This will give you adequate time between pumping. If you are purchasing a boat, check to see if the holding tank size is suitable to the plans you have for the boat. Also, verify that the tank is properly installed with vent and pump-out connection. (See Figure 2:3 Legal System for Waste Management.) Note that the vent is important.

If you are installing your own tank or replacing an existing tank, here are some things to consider doing:

- Place the tank in a location that is out of the way but readily accessible to be worked on.
- Install the intake line 1 ½ inch flexible sewage line from the toilet to the top or top of the side of the tank. This will allow you keep pumping into the holding tank until it is full.
- Install the pump-out line from the bottom or bottom of the side of the holding tank to the deck fitting. This will enable you to pump out all or most of the waste from it.
- Install a vent tube from the top of the holding tank to an exhaust fitting (available at marine stores) toward the bow of the boat on the outside of the rail.

Make sure that the vent line is secured in an ever-ascending line. This will keep the line empty of water or waste, enabling the tank to breathe. Be sure that no loops develop which could retain water and block the line. Remember that when you are sailing the boat will heel or be struck with large waves allowing water to enter the vent line. You want this water to drain into the tank leaving the line open.

There are several waste systems on the market that use electricity or chemicals to render the waste acceptable for disposal overboard. I'm afraid that none of these has been universally accepted, and you might find yourself in a jurisdiction that will fine you heavily and make your life miserable. The only other option is the port-a-potty (self-containing) toilet. This is generally accepted, but the capacity is limited and the difficulty of disposing of the contents is inconvenient and messy at best.

The head also has a sink and a hand shower. While on cruise in New England where it tends to be cooler we wash ourselves with wash cloths rather than shower on board. And when we anchor in small secluded bays Down East, we jump in the water. Another option is a couple of times during a cruise, we stay in a marina or a yachting club, renting a mooring or dock space. These establishments have facilities such as showers and laundries. Some of these are quite elaborate, and others are Spartan. However, in either case it is great feeling to take a hot shower after sailing for few days.

So that is more-or-less all you need to know about the inside and the outside of a boat. As I said at the beginning of the chapter, each boat will be a little different but in general all will have the same features put together perhaps in slightly different ways. And remember not to get bogged down trying to memorize a bunch of new terms and concepts. Experiential learning over time is a better way to layer on new knowledge and skills, slowly building up expertise. Keep a text on board you can refer to from time-to-time to look up pertinent information as you need it. And if you are a visual learner, rather than an audio learner, slip a small notebook in your pocket and every so often jot down questions or terms you want to learn about later.

Chapter Three

Beginning the Sailing Season

Each spring Tom and I go through the ritual of preparing *Makai* for the summer sailing season and taking it down the Piscataqua River from Great Bay to Pepperrell Cove (see Great Bay 70.877 west longitude 43.071 north latitude). The season really begins in March or April when Tom, chomping at the bit, impatiently waits for the New Hampshire snow to melt so that he can hurry to the marina and strip the tarps off the boat. In the fall Tom builds a wooden cradle around the boat and then covers it with several huge tarps. This protects it from the sun, snow, ice, and pests such as birds and other animals that like to find a home in the snug dry boat during the cold months. After we take the tarps off, fold them for storage, and break down the cradle, we give the boat an initial examination. It usually looks grimy, but solid.

Tom's next big project is getting the diesel engine up and going. If there are no problems, he simply changes the oil. Then he test-runs the engine. It takes a bit of effort to do this when the boat is not in the water because the engine requires cooling when it is running. There is a water pump in the engine for this purpose, and it has a hose connected to a through-hull fitting through which cold salt water is sucked. This water passes through the engine and is ejected out of the boat with the exhaust. On land Tom rigs up a system with a short hose connecting the engine's water pump to a large five-gallon pail full of water that has a garden hose running to the marina water supply. Once the engine engages, it draws the water from the bucket through the short hose, and the marina water supply replaces it through the garden hose. Tom runs the engine for about fifteen minutes before shutting it down. He then reconnects the hose from the engine's water pump to the through-hull fitting so it can again such water from the outside when the boat is placed in the water.

By the way, it is a good idea for you to find the "raw-water-intake" fitting (where the water enters the boat) before the boat goes in the water. Take a good look at it and remember its location. When underway, it will, of course, be under water. Also figure out how to access it from inside. The reason I suggest this is because we had several experiences where the raw-water-intake fitting's filter got clogged with seaweed and other detritus. This caused the engine to overheat which could have had disastrous consequences. Tom eventually put a metal grill on the fitting which prevented large debris from getting into the engine.

Next Tom goes on to work on the water system, draining out the antifreeze and filling the water tank with fresh water. Then he reconnects all of the hoses that were disconnected during the winter and allows the system to build up pressure. Water tanks are far more important than one would normally think. *Makai's* tank holds a hundred gallons, and it fills a huge cavity under the floorboards of the main cabin. Ours is made of hard, white plastic, and after we owned the boat for a while, Tom rigged a lift, pulled the tank from its place, and propped it up in the cabin. We then cleaned out the bilge (the part of the boat below the water where the sides curve inward to the keel) and the inside of water tank with a light bleach solution. After that we felt confident that any water stored in the tank was fresh and potable.

A hundred gallons of fresh water is a lot. In fact when Tom told me that is what the tank held, I frankly did not believe him. In a two week cruise, we fill the tank up every three or four days. Where does the water go, I asked myself? We do not shower on board. Rather we depend on sponge baths, wetting a wash cloth and wiping our bodies down. We save our serious bathing for dips in salt water or at marinas where there is plenty of hot water. To brush our teeth, we use one cup of water each (no running water while we brush, like at home). When I do dishes, I fill a pot with soapy water, wash the dishes, and put them in a strainer where I rinse them with clean water heated on the stove. For drinking and cooking water (for pasta, for example), we fill a jug from which we draw during the day and night. Where indeed do those hundred gallons go?

Yet "go" they do. I remember us returning from cruise one summer. We were heading for home, to Pepperrell Cove, and we pulled into Biddeford, Maine where we picked up a mooring in the harbor (70.352 west longitude 43.453 north latitude). Biddeford has a Yacht Club and docks off the harbor in a narrow passageway that leads to a smaller pool beyond the harbor. It was late afternoon, and a fresh breeze had kicked up, making the outer bay's water white and frothy. Our plan was to relax, have dinner, and go to sleep early, hoping to make it to the Cove the next day. I went below to start dinner, and the tell-tale sound of the stalled water pump alerted us to the bad news. I lifted the floorboards and stuck my hand in the water tank to find it empty. When had we last filled the tank?

We decided to try to approach the docks to get water. Dropping our mooring, we headed to the narrow passage way to their dock. But the winds and currents defeated us, and after several attempts between us and the well-meaning people on the dock, we returned to our mooring. Realizing it was late and the Yacht Club was shutting down (and we still had no water), we radioed in, and they sent out a launch. I jumped into the little boat, which was bouncing around in the wind and waves, and we managed to get to the dock. I filled the empty water bottles as I had carried with me as quickly as I could, and we sped back over the waves to *Makai*. That night we at least had cooking and drinking water, even if we missed our sponge baths.

Holding tanks, described in Chapter Two, are another indispensable part of the marine system that needs maintaining. At the beginning of the season Tom fills the tank with water and a cleaning agent to be pumped out at a licensed pump-out station prior to departing the marina. It is illegal to dispose of human waste into rivers or the ocean. Waste needs to be pumped out properly and legally.

Another critical task involves sanding and painting the underside of the boat with anti-fouling paint. The bottom of the boat is underwater for several months of each year, and weeds and barnacles attach themselves, causing what is called "fouling" which results in a considerable loss of boat performance. This is a long-standing problem for sailors. Back in the 1800s Captain Ferdinand Gravert, born in what is today Germany, invented one of the first anti-fouling paints. These paints have evolved over time. Tom still remembers when they required a full sanding of the bottom of the boat and the application of toxic compounds over the entire underside of the boat. The compound prevented the growth of marine organisms, but it also damaged the environment. Today there are paints that minimize sanding and involve the gradual release of the protective substances, which are not so harmful. There are even products that advertise themselves as "green" (ecologically safe) versions of paint that are safe and easy to apply. And they clean up with just soap and water. Tom usually chooses a cool day to do this messy job. It is hot and dirty work. He wears coveralls, goggles, a special hat, and gloves. He sands the parts of the boat bottom that need it, and then covers those patches with those ingredients that keep the hull clear of fouling during the sailing season.

Because Tom really loves his boat, each year he makes at least one improvement on it. He does such things as replacing the vinyl and wood surfaces in the cabins, varnishing the insides of the cabin, fixing the hot water heater, rebuilding the mainsheet traveler (a sliding fixture attached to a track that enables the mainsheet to be eased quickly in gusts), upgrading the stove, and repairing sails.

One year he put his mind to solving a long-standing problem with *Makai's,* unenclosed propeller which is particularly susceptible to picking up the lobster pot lines that litter the mouths of harbors and river mouths. During the winter Tom designed a clever gadget that would protect the propeller from picking up any more pots. This was described in Chapter One.

One of Tom's last chores, with which I help him, is putting the sails on the boat. First we put on the mainsail and then the headsail which must be attached to its roller- furling system. This concept, which has been around since the early 1900s, was only perfected for general use in the 1980s. The headsail is wound around a tube, which, when rotated, either furls it (winds up the sail) or reefs it (lets out the appropriate amount of sail in the wind). We then bring aboard the monitors for the electronics which we keep at home during the winter. These include the monitors for the mapping GPS and the radar. We also reinstall the paddle-wheel speed sensor in its through-hull fitting in the bow of the boat. I am sometimes asked to spin this wheel from inside the boat when we are underway to make sure it functions.

Tom doesn't see working on the boat as drudgery. He really enjoys going out to the marina where he loves being out in the sunshine and warm air and talking to other boaters who compare notes and share sea stories. Over the years he has developed casual friendships with many of the men who own the boats that are stored near ours when it is on the land.

SIDE BAR 3:1 TOOLS AND SPARE PARTS

Tom is fond of saying (usually when I'm fighting him for drawer space in the main cabin) that it is nice to imagine an extended cruise on your boat without anything going wrong. He says that this may be a pleasant dream, but it generally has little to do with reality. Your boat is very much like a space ship…a self-contained survival capsule. When on the sea, there are no hardware stores around, so you must be prepared for pretty much of anything. In order to keep your boat functioning you need tools, parts and knowledge of its workings.

Tom suggests that you should have the following tools:

- Electrical multi-meter (digital) to check voltages, loads, continuity, etc.
- Wrenches (open, box, socket, Allen) (SAE and Metric).
- Screwdrivers (flat and Phillips) of all sizes.
- Vise grips (several sizes).
- Pipe wrenches (to handle big jobs like thru-hull fittings).
- Small wood saw and metal (hack) saw.
- Hand-held drill and rechargeable drill, and lots of drill bits.
  Equip your boat with an inverter to provide 120V AC power from your battery. This is essential for recharging phones, computers, drills etc. (See Side Bar 4:3.)
- Long magnetic retriever (magnet attached to a flexible rod to pick up dropped things from unreachable places).
- Several metal coat hangers. These can be made into long wires with hooks to unblock lines, fish wires, retrieve things from the bilge or elsewhere, etc.
- Good quality string and waxed string for use in rope work.

- Several sharp knives (one that is REALLY heavy and sharp for cutting through rope under water).
- Strong epoxy cement.
- Good quality 12V vacuum cleaner with hose and attachments.
- Two pairs of good quality scissors.
- Many good-quality flashlights liberally sprinkled all over your boat.
- A kerosene lantern and unscented lamp oil which was our preferred way of lighting the main cabin at night. It saved battery power.

As for spare parts:

- Spare fuses for all in use.
- Spare impellers for all pumps on the boat.
- Lots of SS hose clamps of all sizes. They may save your life.
- Nuts, bolts, screws washers of every type. Tom keeps a plastic tool box filled with all sorts of fasteners, and it pays off.
- Marine hose of varying size and connectors.
- Spools of electrical wire (several gauges).
- Wire connectors and tool (several sizes).
- Electrical tape (black and white) and rigging tape.
- SS Shackles of varying sizes and blocks.
- Sail repair kit (needles, high quality thread, patching tape, and sail cloth).
- If you are contemplating a long cruise, consider investing in a small portable generator. If your diesel line becomes air bound, it doesn't take too long before you have depleted your batteries in the process of bleeding the lines. Crank up the generator and recharge your batteries. Otherwise, rely on your sails; they are the ultimate spare part.

I don't enjoy working on the boat as much as Tom does. I see it more like housework – something that is necessary and enjoyed when it is over. One of my major responsibilities is to sand and varnish the wood work which is referred to as "brightwork." Brightwork is a never-ending challenge. When Tom and I first got *Northstar* I was so excited that I spent a week stripping the wooden sides of the cockpit and the edges of the companionway. This in and of itself was a task for which I was unprepared. I started by sanding by hand, then switched to using a sanding machine, and finally used a chemical remover. Days later I finished.

When all the surfaces were clean of the dull, chipped varnish, I taped the edges of the woodwork with generic masking tape to protect the fiberglass cockpit surfaces from seeping and spillage. This turned out to be a bad move because when I finally finished varnishing days later, I could not remove the tape. It took me hours of picking at it before I learned that applying mineral spirits to it would have allowed me to peel it off more easily. Now I use special painters' masking tape, and I strip it off the same day I put it on. I usually apply the tape and the varnish in the morning and pull it off before I leave the marina in the late afternoon.

Another un-fun mistake I made had to do with applying a second coat of varnish. The first time I worked on *Northstar's* brightwork, I put on a coat of marine varnish and, in an effort to avoid sanding between coats, I put on a second coat before the first was completely dry. The surfaces immediately blistered. With dismay I sanded off the blisters and began again. This time I waited a day for the first coat of varnish to dry completely before sanding and applying a second coat.

For two years I decided to avoid sanding and varnishing all together by using an oil that is applied directly to the sanded wood. The instructions said to put on three or four coats of oil each year to protect the surfaces. This in fact did allow me to avoid sanding; however, I had to put on more coats of oil than I did varnish. Plus the oil wore off more quickly than the varnish so that, by the end of the sailing season, the exposed wood took a beating from the salt water and the sun. And I never did like the matte finish of the oil as much as I liked the shininess of the varnished-covered teak. So I eventually switched back to varnish.

Over the years I developed a system of caring for the wood so that now I do not mind doing the brightwork so much. I take a couple of hours of day one to sand *Makai's* toe-rail, the horseshoe-shaped frame which surrounds the cockpit, and cockpit moldings. After I sand, I wipe the surfaces clean with a damp cloth. The next day I return and put the first coat of varnish on. Day three I spend about two hours sanding and wiping again, and day four I finish up by applying a second coat of varnish. About every five years, Tom and I work together to strip all the surfaces and really clean the wood well. Then we put on two coats of fresh varnish.

I think I have made every mistake that one could possibly make as I learned about working on brightwork. The knowledge I have has been hard won. But I really love the look of the boat once its wood is all clean and shiny, so, to my mind, all the work is worth it.

I also clean and wax the topsides. I used to do the entire topsides of *Northstar* myself, but *Makai* is ten feet longer (74 feet of surface if you count both sides) so Tom starting helping me. At one point, thinking they looked dinghy, he decided to redo them. Over the years he refinished all of the topsides using brilliant-white two-part epoxy paint so that the boat looks like new.

I also wipe down all of the surfaces of the inside cabins with a part-bleach solution to rid it of any mildew that might have formed over the cold wet winter. Each year I found fewer and fewer patches, so I gradually won the battle. The last thing to be done is for me to make sure that the galley is stocked with food; the dishes, pots and pans, and cutlery are clean; the head has soap and toilet paper, etc.; and the forward cabin has bedding and clothes stored in the drawers. At this point I always feel like I am rushing because we set a date for the boat to be put in the water but we are rarely ready when the time arrives. The evening before the boat is to be put in the water usually finds us frantically at work finishing last-minute chores.

SIDE BAR 3:2 STOCKING THE GALLEY

Neither *Trull II* nor *Northstar* had proper galleys. They had sinks, and we purchased a camp stove to use with propane gas for *Northstar*. Everything was informal, and we ate out a lot or brought in prepared food. This is certainly one way to approach eating-on-board, and we have known sailing-families who served cold cereal in the morning and ate out for all other meals, and it worked for them.

However, *Makai* has a "real" galley with a stove and an oven, an ice chest, a double sink, and countertops. The icebox opens from the top, so it gets very cold in the bottom, allowing us to store fresh meat and chicken there for up to three days. On

---

the upper shelves where it isn't quite as cold, we keep eggs, butter, and some leafy fresh vegetables. I have a tiny hammock that I hang high above one of the main-cabin couches where I keep lettuce (cut out the core; the head lasts longer that way) and other fresh vegetables (squashes, carrots, zucchini, sweet potatoes, and onions which last longer than leafy vegetables).

On long weekends we use the oven and stove top, but when cruising we avoid cooking with the oven because it uses up too much propane gas. Instead we switch to stove-top-roasting which works very well. As I have mentioned before, the stove is gimbaled. It remains upright even when the boat heels while underway or when it bounces around on anchor.

I write up a galley inventory at the beginning of each season, shop for goods, and stock the galley. I keep in my purse or knapsack a running list of what supplies I need to replenish and replace them from time to time. We always have plenty of canvas bags on board to take to shops and grocery stores. After a couple of seasons Tom and I invested in a metal roller-basket for carrying large bundles of food. I remember it was particularly helpful when we shopped for groceries in Pemaquid, Maine after being under sail and away from towns for a while. The grocery store we finally found was over a mile from the place we moored the boat, and we ended up trudging there and back with the roller-basket making a real contribution.

I have known sailing women who baked their own bread and cooked elaborate meals each day. Tom and I lay somewhere between these intrepid women and the cereal-in-the-morning/eat-out-for-dinner families. We both like to cook, so we've tried many dishes on board. Breakfast for us begins with coffee or tea. We use an old-fashioned percolator and perk the coffee for at least three minutes like my mother and aunt used to do. This process not only produces flavorful coffee, but it also kills any bacteria that may be in the water. Then we prepare either cold or hot cereal or toast (toasted on a camp toaster over the gas jet) and eggs.

I remember waking up early one morning when we had a mooring in Biddeford Pool. The sun had not yet rose, and I sat out in the cockpit with a cup of coffee, luxuriating in the quiet, still morning. It turned hot after the sun came up, and for breakfast we had cold cereal with milk and fruit. Another cold, clammy morning in Portland when the fog was so thick we couldn't see the boat moored next to us, we made hot oatmeal and spooned strawberry jam and sour cream on top it.

While we usually use our camp toaster to make toast, we also make it by frying bread in butter or oil. Below I have included a recipe that is a bit more elaborate for a lay-over-day brunch, or it is versatile enough to serve as a dinner, depending on how you "dress it up."

Makai French Toast

Four pieces of whole wheat bread.

Dip into a batter of:

- Two well-beaten eggs
- Half a cup of half-and-half or milk
- Teaspoon of salt
- Tablespoon of sugar
- Half a teaspoon of cinnamon and nutmeg

Fry in butter or oil until browned.

After dipping each of the four pieces of bread, if there is still eggy batter left, pour it over the last pieces of bread as they cook. It will make a custard-like dish.

Serve with sour cream and strawberry, raspberry, or blueberry jam, or with butter and syrup.

Note: This dish is gentle enough on the stomach to have as dinner after a rough sail. Or you can add bacon and/or ham to it to make it even more substantial for an evening meal. It can be thrown together quickly, should people be tired and ready to sleep.

Some choices for lunch include a variety of soups which can be eaten from mugs in the cockpit while underway. These are much appreciated on cold afternoons while sailing. Tuna-fish salad or chicken salad sandwiches are always popular. I stock the galley with at least 10 cans of tuna and chicken for a two-week cruise. Canned tuna or chicken can also be mixed with pasta for a dinner. One tip Tom and I received from a sailing couple was that once you open a jar of mayonnaise, you don't need to refrigerate it (as I do at home) unless you contaminate it with a spoon or fork. We did this for years and found that it worked. Peanut-butter-and-jelly sandwiches are an excellent stand-by. And it is always easy to throw together a quick lunch of left-over beef, chicken, or whatever we had the night before in a salad with a simple vinaigrette.

I always keep plenty of saltine crackers and pretzels on board to fight seasickness. They reduce stomach acid. This being said, I have to add that Tom prefers beer, reasoning the carbonated drink gives relief by causing belching.

Tom and I feel deprived if we don't have a nice dinner, so we both put extra thought into this meal's preparation. Over the years, we, like countless other couples, have developed sets of recipes that work particularly well on the boat and that are nourishing and tasty. We always try to cook extra so there are left-overs for lunch the next day.

Essential carbohydrate staples for the galley are pasta, rice, and potatoes. To create variety I also have on board prepared items, including bags of pasta in different sauces that you just boil and serve. As I mentioned above, a can of tuna or chicken can be mixed in at the last moment. We stock canned vegetables, especially small cans of mushrooms which can be added to just about anything including omelets and pasta. A red wine sauce for beef and canned or bottled spaghetti sauce are also versatile. Condiments such as mustard, mayonnaise, honey, and ketchup as well as herbs, spices, salt, and pepper are important. We do not take bottled salad dressings with us on cruise, mixing our own vinaigrette instead, which is made of one part wine vinegar, three parts olive oil, one half a teaspoon of mustard, a teaspoon of honey, salt, and pepper to taste.

For protein sources, besides canned tuna or chicken, we store in the bottom of the ice box fresh chicken and meat that we consume in about three or four days. We plan on eating out at least every few days. Tom invented a great chicken recipe that we use a great deal while cruising.

> ### *Makai Mustard Chicken*
>
> Two bone-in chicken breasts, salted on both sides.
>
> Mix two tablespoons of Grey Poupon Dijon Mustard with three tablespoons of mayonnaise.
>
> Slather the mixture on the two chicken breasts.
>
> Sprinkle paprika on them.
>
> Either bake in an oven or stove-bake (covered) on a burner for about 45 minutes, depending on how hot your oven or burner gets.

Tom discovered that *Makai* has a small locker in the aft cabin that is suited for storing wine. We stock it with a variety of boxes of white and red wines that we drink with dinner. He also stores beer in a locker in the cockpit which he keeps cold with ice blocks from marinas.

SIDE-BAR 3:3 THE HEAD AS A "MEDICINE CABINET"

The "medicine cabinet" in people's homes often serves as a place for hygienic and first-aid products. You may want to rethink this if your head is far from the galley and the cockpit where accidents might happen. If this is the case, keep in the head only hygienic items, and store the first-aid kit (discussed under the Side Bar 4:2 Safety) in the cockpit or near the companionway.

In our head lockers we stock common items frequently found in everyone's medicine cabinet. The list is not meant to be comprehensive, but only to make a few suggestions. These include:

- Toothbrushes, tooth paste, and dental floss – to conserve water, expect to use one glass of water to brush, rinse, and clean your tooth brush.
- Soap and a washcloth – on cruise we sponge-bathed, wash in the sea, or use the bathing facilities at marinas and yacht clubs. Bring bags for men and for women to take to the showers in case the showers are segregated by gender.
- Shampoo, conditioner, comb, brush – items for hair cleaning and care.
- Small and medium-sized towels. Several changes depending on length of cruise and how fastidious people are.
- Nail-clippers, Emery boards, nail brush.
- Lotion, face cream, and extra-heavy hand lotion for dried hands. In New England the cold, even in the summer, takes its toll on the skin, especially on the hands that pull on lines and clench the wheel for hours at a time (even if you are wearing gloves).
- Vaseline (it has so many uses), Chap Stick with sun block in it (many people forget to coat their lips with sun block and regret it later)
- Sun block. I struggled for years with applying various kinds of block and using any number of products, including white zinc, especially on my nose. I have had pre-cancerous spots burned off my nose three times to date in spite of my efforts. Use a hat, stay covered as best you can, and use the best sun block you can find to protect your skin.
- Tylenol, Aleve, aspirin, etc. Stock a bottle of whichever analgesic you and your family members usually use for the aches and pains that are caused by the stresses and strains of the exercise you experience while sailing and being in the sun.
- Antihistamines and/or decongestants which can alleviate the symptoms of allergies from Maine's pine trees, bug bites, incipient colds, etc.
- Bug spray of some kind to protect you against insect bites.
- Pepto-Bismol and/or Kaopectate for diarrhea and nausea.
- Cortisone ointment for bug bites and poison ivy.
- Dramamine or other anti-motion-sickness medicines. I used Dramamine for years in spite of it making me sleepy. I also used pressure-wrist bracelets which didn't work for me. Then I switched to scopolamine patches that I place in back of my ears. I have found them to be helpful in that although I sense the bouncing and rolling of the boat, I don't feel like throwing up.

- Prescription medicines you normally take. I would advise you taking extra doses in case you get delayed somewhere. Also take the telephone number of your primary-care physician and your pharmacy. I remember being in Portland, Maine and needing more scopolamine patches. The pharmacist there called my pharmacist at home who cordially arranged a refill with my physician in less time than it took me to explain this.

Of course everyone's medicine cabinet contains things that are unique to specific families and individuals. The above list is meant only to help you compile your own inventory.

The boat normally goes in the water at the end of May unless Tom is working on an exceptionally large project. If that is the case, it goes in the water at the end of June. The staff at the marina has equipment that lifts up huge *Makai* (fifteen tons) and carries it to the river banks where they drop it into the river. When they have placed the boat on a mooring in Great Bay, they contact us, and we mobilize. The first thing we need to do is leave one of the cars at the parking lot near the public dock in Kittery Point where we will arrive the following day. Then we drive back to the marina and leave another car there. Tied to the car's roof is the dingy, and the dingy engine is in the trunk. We used to laboriously half-drag and half-carry the dinghy down the dock to the water. But now we just back the car down the public boat ramp and push the dinghy in the water. Once it is in, we park the car and load the dinghy engine and cooler that holds fresh food into the waiting dinghy. Then we take off for *Makai*.

A feeling of exhilaration fills me as we speed over the water. Tom and I look forward to spending at least one night on the mooring in tranquil Great Bay and feel cheated if it rains or if it is too cold for us to enjoy sitting out. That first night is an ideal time for us is to sit in the cockpit and watch the birds soar above the water. The sounds from the marina are dim in the background when we go down under and prepare dinner in the main cabin. As I work at the stove I look out the porthole and see the banks of the bay where great blue herons fish.

After dinner we go back to the cockpit and leisurely sip coffee while we listen to music. If we are really lucky, it is hot enough for us to jump off the back of the boat. If there is no moon and no one visible on the shore or in other moored boats, we skinny-dip without worrying about being seen. The river-bay water is warm compared to the chilly ocean water, and there have been times when I have not wanted to get out and dry off before going to bed. When we climb into our bunk, we hear only the birds' cries and the sound of the current gently washing against the hull.

Great Bay is an enchanted place, and I love it there. I have never dreamed about having a home on the ocean, finding the sound of the waves and the wind too restless for my liking. But I would really like a home on a bay. The tranquility of the trees and water coupled with the wide-open spaces and the sound of the birds are beautiful.

The next morning Tom and I are up early to have coffee in the cockpit and watch for low tide. To get down the river to our mooring we need to go under four bridges. Two are lift bridges, and we radio the bridge men to raise them at their designated time. The other two are fixed bridges, and one of these we can only go under at low tide. This bridge is nearest to the marina, so we wait for the low tide or a reading of 52-feet on the bridge scale before we beginning our trip down the river. The next fixed bridge is the huge Interstate-95 bridge which goes from New Hampshire to Maine. Its clearance is 155 feet so there is no problem for our 50-foot mast.

There is always a surge of anxiety as we go under the first fixed bridge named the General Sullivan Bridge. We have known people who have had their masts hit it, which, frankly, it is not an experience I want to have. In addition sometimes the current is not exactly slack when we leave the mooring. The water is still rushing out to the sea which creates a strong current that can push the boat sideways, especially when the water is funneled though the bridge supports.

Once when we went under the bridge we saw (and heard) the top of the wind vane, which reaches about a foot above the mast, hit the bridge. That was definitely a close call. Another time I was on the wheel, taking the boat beneath the bridge, when to my horror I felt the boat slide sideways and make for one of the stone bridge supports. To make matters worse there was a small power boat which was not faring much better than we were in the current. Neither of us was in control of our boats, and I was afraid I would hit either the bridge or the boat. I called out to Tom for help, and he managed to adjust *Makai's* course, missing the powerboat and safely passing beneath the bridge.

Another time a large power yacht came right toward us, in the center of the channel under the bridge, pressing us to the side of the channel. Only frantic signaling by us got the captain of the boat to realize he had to move over and let us have the center of the channel where the bridge clearance is at its maximum. He could pass easily on either side of the center, but *Makai*, with its 50-foot mast, could not.

Yet another time we were with another couple bringing the boat up the river, and it turned dark and foggy by the time we arrived at the bridge. As we crept along from marker to marker we listened carefully for the sound of other boats. Every now and then one of us blasted the hand-held horn to let people know our position. I was very nervous that night, and when the bridge loomed above us, I definitely felt fear. But everything worked out just fine. We later had twelve lobsters between the four of us in a local restaurant.

The trip down river is always more relaxed after we leave those fixed bridges behind us. We spend the next hour and a half leisurely enjoying the wooded shores and clusters of houses, watching the birds, and waving to other boaters who pass us. We reach the lovely city of Portsmouth towards the end of our trip. Tom or I radio the Sarah Long Bridge, asking to be let through at the appropriate time. Soon we hear sirens as the traffic is stopped. Then the bridge rises slowly to let us serenely pass beneath it. For about a quarter of an hour we remain between the Sarah Long and Memorial Bridges. We circle off the Portsmouth docks admiring the restaurants and the newly renovated buildings. It is an attractive town with a lot of energy. Then the Memorial Bridge lifts, and we pass under it. After each bridge we radio a thank you to the man or woman who carefully scrutinizes us as we motor by in the river beneath them.

Photo 3:1 Tom, *Makai,* River, Bridge
Tom on *Makai,* taking the sailboat down the river to Pepperrell Cove.

After the bridges there is not a lot of the trip left. We pass by the Portsmouth Shipyard with its huge empty prison on the bluff and the submarines lying on the docks being worked on. Then we turn the corner, and the ocean breeze catches us as we head toward Pepperrell Cove (see 70.704 west longitude 43.077 north latitude). Usually I grab a sweater at this point because it is invariably much colder off of Kittery Point than it is in Great Bay.

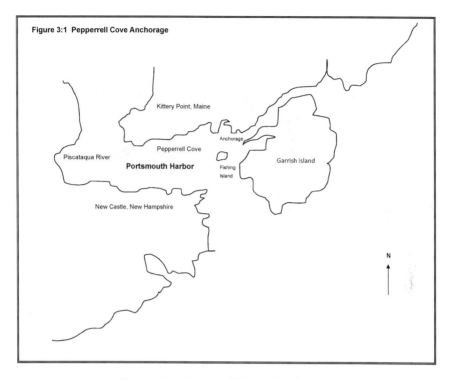

Figure 3:1 Pepperrell Cove Anchorage

Kittery Point, Maine

Anchorage

Pepperrell Cove

Piscataqua River

Portsmouth Harbor

Fishing
Island

Garrish Island

New Castle, New Hampshire

N

Figure 3:1 Pepperrell Cove Anchorage

Our mooring has already been serviced by a mooring-maintenance firm before we start down the river. We motor towards it, and Tom moves forward with the pick-up pole to retrieve the mooring lines. Invariably they are all slimy and foul from being in the water for several weeks. Sometimes, if the wind is strong, we need to circle around several times before it is possible to approach the mooring ball at a reasonable speed. Tom grabs the lines and attaches them to the cleats as I move forward with a pail of water and a brush. We do our best to clean them off so that they do not dirty the bow of the boat too much. Then we wash off our own hands which smell pungently of the sea.

Photo 3:2 Pepperrell Cove view
Pepperrell Cove's views are beautiful. The cove is shared by working
lobstermen, recreational powerboaters, kayakers, and sailors.

The trip down the river in the spring marks the beginning of the
summer sailing season. As Tom and I go through the familiar routine
we need to remind ourselves of things half-forgotten. It is like getting
on a horse after not having ridden for a while. Motoring at the correct
speed toward the mooring, using the pick-up pole, watching out for the
markers so we do not get in water that is two shallow, remembering to
pass boats port to port, monitoring the compass and the wind speed/
direction indicator (even if it is not entirely accurate in that it reads too
high), and using the hand-held and regular two-way radio are all tasks
that we need to relearn. We both look forward to this first time on the
boat and all that the summer season promises.

SIDE BAR 3:4 LEAVING THE BOAT ALONE ON ITS MOORING

While preparing the boat to go in the water, Tom and I make a list of things we need to remember to do before we leave the boat alone on its mooring in Pepperrell Cove. It makes sense to do this while you are getting the boat ready and refreshing your memory from last season rather than when you are on your mooring, five minutes from locking up the boat and getting into your dinghy to leave for a week or two.

Shut the engine down and leave the gearshift left in neutral position with the pin that engages the transmission in the unengaged position (*Makai* has a button; unengaged for it is the "out" position). The transmission needs to be unengaged so that when you return to the boat and turn on the engine, then the transmission doesn't automatically engage and move the boat forward or in reverse. This is much like a car which, when turned off, is left in "park."

Remove the boat's starter key from the ignition and store it away or take it with you. You'd be surprised how many times we have forgotten the key and left it in the cockpit for anyone to pick up. Check the oil level, and if it is low, make a note to bring oil the next time you are on the boat. The batteries must be turned off. This should not affect the automatic bilge pump (the pump that removes any water from the bottom of the boat) which is wired directly to one of the batteries.

The valves which control water intake must be shut. This includes the seacocks on the engine raw-water intake, the galley sink drain, and the head-intake valve which allows you to pump water into the head for flushing waste into the holding tank. Closing the ports and the hatches securely not only prevents people from entering the boat but protects the boat from rains and other consequences of bad weather.

Switch off the electronic equipment. You won't need the depth finder on while you are away from the boat. Remove items from the cockpit and store them in the main cabin. The cushions, pillows, winch handles, maps, charts, sun block, and any other gear need to be stowed. Secure everything inside the boat. Nothing should be left out because if the boat is tossed about on its mooring, then things might break. Most boats have lockers in which dishes, pots and pans, charts, books, and items in the head can be safely stored. It's important to use them.

Whether you are coming home after a long cruise or a short day's outing, make sure that the ice box and the cockpit cooler are empty, cleaned out, and wiped down. This is particularly important after a passage when you might have stored raw chicken and meat in the ice box. Leave the lids open so the compartments can breathe, but jammed so that they don't bounce around should there be turbulence. We leave the ice box lid and a storage area lid propped up in the two sinks.

All of the sails must be furled tightly. The sail cover should be tied on the mainsail which has been secured on top of the boom. This protects the sail from sun damage. Especially in the late summer, we cover the boom, dodger, and cockpit with a tarp that protected them from the laughing gulls who tend to sit on the boom and soil the area around them. We also tie off the halyards so that they don't clank against each other when the boat lists from side to side on the mooring. This is a matter of courtesy in that the halyards may be music to our ears, but others may think they make a racket. Coil all the lines so they don't fly about or land in the water, and hang coiled lines wherever possible. We always hang the coiled mainsail sheet from the boom at the end of the day.

Bundle up any trash to take with you. And, remember to take keys, wallets, purses, and bags with you. More than once we have returned from a cruise and forgot the keys to the car. Tom and I dinghy to the dock, carefully tie off the dinghy, trudge up to the parking lot, and realize we have forgotten the keys. Back we go to the boat.

Over the years, our list has grown. And we have plasticized it and tacked it to the board in the galley where we can easily see it and mentally check off the tasks before we leave. Not only does this ensure that we sleep easy while at home knowing the boat is safe while we are not there, but Tom and I know what to expect when we return to the boat. We'll have power; the bilge will be empty; the cushions will be dry; the mainsail and dodger will not smell of guano; and so on.

Chapter Four

Intangibles and Tangibles: Bringing What You Need on Board

Intangibles

Sometimes sailing involves Zen-like discipline. It requires you to strip down to the absolute necessities and focus, above all, focus. A correct mindset is indispensable, if you expect to be successful and to enjoy yourself. Whether making a two-week passage or out sailing for the afternoon, I try to remember several principles which contribute to having a positive sailing experience.

The first has to do with emptying your mind of all bothersome thoughts. Leave work or home troubles behind before climbing on board and fill your mind with sailing-related thoughts. Usually this is not hard to do because there are so many things going on while on board that ruminating becomes impossible. Concentrating on adjusting the sails, setting the GPS device, or dropping an anchor take over.

There is something about the sea and winds that allows me to forget the concerns that seemed so overwhelming on land. Maybe it's the rhythm of the waves that dispels the tensions that are brought on board. Or maybe the pure beauty of the vistas and animals crowds out all negative thoughts. I know that the first time I saw whales around our boat I was thunderstruck. First of all, they were bigger than our boat, which gave me pause. But mostly, I was amazed by their grace. It is really hard to stay annoyed with a work colleague while you are enthralled by watching a whale come up, exhale steam, and then inhale air before rolling back down into the deep. Mundane sailing tasks also demand your attention. Trimming the sails so that their bellies aren't luffing but taut, checking the compass to make sure you're on course, searching for the next waypoint---all these activities require a sailor to be alert and focused at all times.

Another principle has to do with sailing-being-fun. Sailing, to my mind, is not supposed to be a cut-throat competitive experience or an opportunity for a captain to yell at the crew and make them feel stupid. Certainly I have been on or near boats where competition or anger were clearly the central focus, but Tom and I have not embraced either of those models. Having said that, I know that some people find sailboat racing to be the best fun there is. Many of the yacht clubs that we have visited as transients organize races regularly. That is another thing entirely. People engage in this activity for the purpose of competing; it is a sport. The kind of negative competition I'm talking about is when this quality inappropriately enters into a non-sport event, an event where rivalry has no place. Once we were cruising in Casco Bay with a group of friends, and the captain of one of the boats spoiled the afternoon by becoming enraged because their boat was constantly behind everyone else's. The crew clearly suffered, and so did the rest of us indirectly.

Good manners go a long way on a boat where close-living over weeks can sometimes lead to irritation and tempers flaring. Although Tom and I are usually very good about observing proper etiquette, from time to time, difficulties occur. For example, I sometimes feel panicky when Tom suddenly changes his mind about something I have to do. For example, when docking, I put lines on the foredeck and the stern of the boat and fenders on whichever side we are coming in on (port or starboard). This procedure takes about ten minutes or so because I have to get the fenders and lines out of cockpit locker and then put them out. While I do this task, Tom is either approaching the dock or circling around it waiting for a space for *Makai*.

The difficulty arises when he is compelled for reasons outside his control to change his mind about which side we are docking, causing me to rush around the boat switching the lines and the fenders. If he does not give me enough time, it can be harrowing, and I get agitated. I have found that it works best if I keep him informed of what I'm doing. I let him know where the lines and fenders are, and what I need to do if there is a change of plans, since his attention is clearly and necessarily focused on the dock and the other boats around us, and not on the tasks for which I have responsibility.

SIDE BAR 4:1 DOCKING AND MOORING YOUR BOAT

Two essential skills every sailor must learn are how to dock a boat and how to pick up a mooring. Docks and moorings are required in areas that are congested and don't allow anchoring. With docking, more so than mooring, you must know the idiosyncrasies of your boat- how readily the helm turns the boat, whether your boat reverses to port or to starboard, etc. *Makai*, for example, reverses more easily to port. This means that when we want to dock, we must approach with the dock on the port side. This allowed us to secure the boat's bow and reverse the engine bringing the stern of the boat to the dock.

Knowing the direction we want to follow allows us to prepare. Three or four fenders are suspended from the lifeline so as to protect the side of the boat where it will hit the dock. A dock line is uncoiled on the forward deck, and the end is passed over the lifeline and through the port hawserhole and secured to the forward cleat. The line is passed outside of the shrouds and placed mid ship on the cabin top. Another line is passed over the lifeline, around the aft stanchion, and secured to the port cleat aft. This line is then placed near the helmsman in the boat's cockpit.

The boat is then driven toward the dock at an angle that will allow the forward fender to contact the middle of the dock space. This angle depends on wind and current. If a stiff breeze is blowing across the dock on to the boat, the angle will need be steeper. If there is a wind or current pushing the boat toward the dock, the angle can be shallower and the speed reduced. Once alongside the dock, the forward deck hand jumps to the deck with the forward docking line. (If the dock is attended, the line is simply tossed to him/her.) The forward line is passed under the appropriate dock cleat, and the boat is powered in reverse. The forward line should not be cleated or snugged too tight in order to allow the reversing process to occur. With the boat propeller pulling the boat both aft and toward the dock, the forward line can be temporarily cleated and the crew member on the dock can move to receive the aft mooring line from the helmsman.

At this point the engine can be powered down, and the positioning of the boat can take place. Once the lines are secured such that the fenders are taking the chafe, spring lines are attached. These lines prevent the boat from bouncing on the dock. This is only needed if the boat will be on the dock for a prolonged period of time. Spring lines run from the aft winch to the forward cleat on the dock and from a stanchion or shroud base forward of mid ship to the aft cleat on the dock.

In the case of picking up a mooring, wind, current and other boats are paramount considerations. This is particularly true if you are in a mooring area which a local club uses the area for dingy or widgeon races. Or even worse, when full-size sailboats weave amidst moored boats. Or worse still, when you have a so-called expert sailor who insists on sailing up to his/her mooring, rather than motoring to it. They usually make mistakes. We came back to *Makai* one weekend to find the lifeline broken and two stanchions bent. There was no message left by the perpetrator.

Preparing to pick up a mooring is less taxing than docking. If the mooring has an attached pick up-pole, you need only to stand in the pulpit and direct the helmsman to the pole. If there is no pick-up pole, have your boat hook ready to pick up the line attached to the hawser buoy. The amount of speed will depend on the wind and current. Too little speed and the boat will be uncontrollable; too much speed and it will be impossible to pick up the pole or retain it. The helmsman should be ready to reverse just prior to or immediately after the pole is grabbed. The pole is attached by line to the mooring hawser. It will have a loop designed to be attached to your cleat. Pass the loop through the appropriate hawser hole and secure it to the forward cleat. If the mooring has not been used in a while, the hawser can be very dirty. Have your bucket and brush handy to clean the rope, deck, and your hands.

Another example is when we are approaching a mooring. Tom is normally at the bow of the boat, and I am on the wheel. The idea is to very slowly approach the mooring, giving Tom time to either grab the mooring pickup pole or use the boat hook to fish the mooring line out of the water. He then attaches the mooring line to a heavy cleat on the foredeck of the boat. Sometimes this procedure goes like clockwork, but sometimes the current or the wind affects the boat so that I have to give the engine more gas. This gives me more control over the boat, but it requires Tom to pick up the mooring line and attach it faster than he is able. He gets impatient. Once again I have found we handle this best if we keep each other informed of what is happening. If the boat is moving too fast through the water, there is no point in Tom trying to do the impossible and having his arms pulled out of their sockets or his hands hurt by the strain on the ropes. If Tom lets me know he cannot pick up the mooring line, we can always circle around and try again. Sometimes, just remembering we can make a second attempt at something alleviates the pressure.

Yet another principle concerns viewing sailing-as-a-learning-experience where it is safe ("OK") to make mistakes. If a person needs to be totally in charge and the expert at all times, then sailing may not be the place for them (unless they are really experts which is another thing altogether).

On a sailboat, there is always something new to learn. Before giving examples of this, Tom insists I add a caveat. He wants people to remember that some mistakes can be dangerous and destructive. For example, if you are sailing on a broad reach, and you have a lapse of attention, the wind could get behind the mainsail and flip the boom to the other side of the boat, potentially hurting a crew member and damaging the boat. And from chapter one we know that anchors can drag so you have to keep an eye on the boat for a while after first anchoring. So I guess all mistakes are not equal. Some have more consequences than others.

SIDE BAR 4:2 SAFETY

Everyone is in agreement that it is better to prevent an accident rather than deal with one after it happens. One of the scariest things that can happen on a sailboat is a man-overboard. To prevent this from happening, Tom is always firm about the rules of having two people in the cockpit, especially for night sailing, and of having safety harnesses available for each crew member. We store those in the cockpit's locker where we can reach them without leaving the cockpit. Some believe safety harness should be worn at all times during night sailing, when you are in rough water, when the boat is reefed (or when you need to go forward to reef a sail), and when a person is working on deck (Sleight 2001, p. 314). Also life vests that have reflective materials and lights on them are important to have because they allow the person to be seen more easily in the water at night.

If the worst-case-scenario happens, and someone does indeed go overboard, there are three main methods for getting the person back in the boat. These can be practiced beforehand if you would like to train your crew. As soon as someone goes over, the first reflex of everyone on board should be to throw a life-ring with a buoy and pickup pole to the person, along with any cushions that serve as life-preservers. The life-ring should be located somewhere convenient to the cockpit. Ours was a large OSHA-yellow-colored horseshoe located in a harness on the starboard aft side of the boat. It was attached to a buoyed and weighted, six-foot fiberglass pole with a flag. One of the crew should be told to keep their eyes on the person in the water at all times so that you can find them again.

The second step is to stop the boat by pushing the tiller or wheel to leeward (away from the wind). The mainsail then moves to the middle of the boat, and the foresail (jib or genoa) flaps. Keep the foresail cleated, and it becomes backfilled. The mainsail and the foresail, in these positions, should stop the boat because you are essentially hoved-to (a boat at a standstill after the foresail has been backfilled). This gives you time to assess the situation.

Another method is to start the motor as fast as you can, loosen both sails so they flap in the wind, and motor back to the person. Depending on the winds, this might be hazardous. For instance, if the wind is behind you, and you jibe with the mainsail up in your haste to get back to the person, it might damage the boat or hurt someone.

A third method is to sail back to the person by using tacks or jibes to reverse the direction of the boat, allowing you to move back toward the person. The disadvantage of this is that it takes time, and the person watching the individual in the water might lose sight of them or the person in the water might experience hypothermia. In places like Maine, the water is cold even in the summer. Average summer water temperatures off the coast of Portland, Maine are 56 degrees in June, 61 degrees in July, and 62 degrees in August. According to the Personal Flotation Device Manufacturing webpage, in waters between 50 and 60 degrees, after one to two hours, exhaustion or unconsciousness sets in.

However, let's assume you have turned the boat around and approached the person. First, throw them a line. If your boat sits high out of the water, as *Makai* does, it will be very difficult to pull a person up the side of the boat with just a rope. If this is the case, consider purchasing a ready-made sling and tackle that can be used to lift the person from the water. This will make things much easier. Another option is, if your engine is not running, that the person can grab the ladder hanging off the stern of the boat. You can then help them clamber up the ladder and into the boat. However various sources advise keeping the individual away from the stern, fearing them may be hurt by the propeller, should the motor be engaged.

The American Sailing Academy strongly urges you to make sure that every person on board knows how to swim and is comfortable in the water. This is especially important with children. With a man-overboard crisis, knowing how to swim can mean the difference between life and death, even if the person reaches the life ring or life preserver you throw to them.

An appropriate first aid kit is an important part of keeping safe. You can purchase one online for about $140 (at the time I am writing this) from Landfall Navigation. It is called a "Medical Sea Pak First Aid Kit in a Waterproof Case." In it you will find five separate kits (what they call modules). Module 1 is for common problems and contains things such as eye wash and bandages; Module 2 is for cuts and splinters and has gauze pads, bandages, and a rubber tourniquet; Module 3 is for sprains and fractures and contains splints and cold packs; Module 4 is for CPR and burns; and Module 5 is for the crew members' prescription drugs. Please note that the above list is not comprehensive. There are a lot of items in each module. If you would prefer not to spend the money, or you think the Sea Pak is overkill, you can make up your own first aid kit, using Tupperware or Rubbermaid containers and selecting the items you think you will need from the list prepared by Landfall Navigation.

I know that after I sprayed an ankle on the island of Jost Van Dyke in the Virgin Islands, I have insisted that we have plenty of things to help with sprains such as cold packs, Ibuprofen or some kind of anti-inflammatory medicine, and Ace bandages for support.

Sailors may want to carefully read through Maloney's Chapter 11 "Safety Afloat" in the 64th edition of the comprehensive and definitive Chapman Piloting & Seamanship (Maloney 2003, p. 368-407). There is a more recently-published text (Eaton 2013); however, I believe Maloney's chapter is quite excellent. There is something in that chapter for everyone. One suggestion that Tom and I noted had to do with a pre-departure float plan which you leave with a family member or friend before a passage. (They advise you not to try to leave such a plan with the US Coast Guard.) It should include information such as the names of the people on board (with addresses and phone numbers of contact people), a description of the boat, the engine type, planned operations (including departure points, destinations, and routes), marine radio, what safety equipment is on board, and other pertinent information (Maloney 2003, 377).

Finally, make provisions for if you have to abandon ship. Most cruising boats have dinghies which can serve as their life rafts. Organize an emergency pack for your life raft which should include water, energy or power bars, flash lights, flares, first aid supplies, cell phones (preferably in durable water-proof bags), a compass, and reflective blankets which protect you from the heat and the cold. Online you can also find life rafts equipped with everything you might need. This might be unnecessary for many cruising families. However, they are out there to investigate.

Once again, most accidents can be prevented. Make sure the worst never happens.

Yet, on the whole, sailing affords us opportunities for learning new things all the time. You never know everything. When I first began to sail we navigated with charts and a compass. We determined where we were and where we wanted to go; then we calculated how far we needed to go and in which direction. When Tom and I were sailing *Northstar,* we traveled from Kittery Point, Maine to Provincetown, Massachusetts using this technique. The problem with this method is that you never really go in exactly the direction you're aiming. For example, we may have needed to go 180 degrees south, but because of the winds and the current, sometimes we might have been sailing 170 degrees and sometimes 190 degrees. A contributing problem was that we never knew exactly where we were. We estimated where we thought we were, and hopefully verified it if we came upon a bell or whistle that was on our charts, or a landmark from which we could take a bearing. But otherwise we approximated our position.

Then Tom purchased a Loran system, which is a device that depends on the intersection of two or more radio signals to determine a position. In some ways it is a more sophisticated version of the old RDF, radio direction finder, which Tom used occasionally before he met me. The Loran showed us where we actually were in the ocean and gave us a course to follow as well as telling us what course we were actually making. This allowed us to sail with more confidence away from the sight of land or in the fog. It also allowed us to put in waypoints which helped us sail from point to point in the direction we wanted to travel.

The Loran was a relief to have when we took our first trip to Portland, Maine. On the way we stopped at the Isles of Shoals, and Tom set up the Loran. Then we sailed to Biddeford Pool near the mouth of the Saco River (see 70.352 west longitude 43.453 north latitude). We entered the harbor and anchored. Then we entered our location into the Loran data base to use on the trip home. We proceeded on to Portland (see 70.151 west longitude 43.394 north latitude), putting in waypoints all along the way. Once we arrived, fog set in. We spent a few pleasant days exploring the town. Then we became a little anxious because Tom and I had to return to work. We decided to take off and do our best to return to Portsmouth Harbor even though we couldn't see a thing. Using the Loran we were able to successfully make our way southwest along the coast. In fact the Loran was so accurate that in Biddeford we were able to return to precisely where we had anchored on our way east.

Our only really bad moment was pulling into Portsmouth Harbor, still in thick fog, and making for Pepperrell Cove. Unbeknownst to us a huge tanker was leaving port and bearing down on us. He must have seen us in his radar because he blasted us with a loud horn. I panicked, not knowing whether to turn to port or to starboard. Tom kept his head and turned to starboard, away from the rocky coast that is protected by a light house. A gigantic tanker loomed out of the fog and passed by us, far too close for my comfort. But that was not the Loran's fault. Before leaving our mooring in the Cove, we had not yet installed the system, and thus had not entered the coordinates of our Pepperrell Cove mooring. The Loran, with the information it had, guided us safely through the days of pea-soup fog to our home base.

SIDE BAR 4:3 TWO-WAY RADIOS, CELL AND SMART PHONES, AND PERSONAL COMPUTERS

When Tom and I first started sailing, we primarily used a two-way marine radio to contact the outside world. Marine radios are for safety and not for making dinner reservations or for chatting. (Once while motoring down the Annisquam River-Canal, I heard a long conversation between two men about the divorce one of them was going through. This was not an appropriate use of the marine radio.) The radio is theoretically supposed to be on all the time in order to listen for distress calls, although ours is sometimes off when we run the engine because the engine noise drowns out the radio. Tom mounted it in the companionway under the dodger for protection from the elements. To use it, you turn it on and spin a knob to find the channel you want. Sixteen is the emergency frequency. Thirteen is to call bridges such as the ones of the Piscataqua River when we take the boat up and down the river. When communicating with another boat or when calling for a yacht club launch, we use the 68 channel. These channels can change, so before using a two-way radio it is best to verify what channels are used for which purposes.

When life or property are in danger, then you can summon help by using the 16 channel as Tom did on our first date. There is something of a formula to this procedure.

- You repeat into the microphone (three times), "Mayday, Mayday, Mayday."
- You give your boat name three times.
- You give your latitude and longitude positions. If you have GPS, this is very easy, and you can give precise information.
- You describe your emergency and what kind of assistance you need.
- You give the number of people on board, report if anyone has been injured, and the kinds of safety equipment you have on board. From personal experience with the US Coast Guard, I can tell you that the first thing they will ask is whether or not you have your life preserver on, so you might as well put it on before you start transmitting.
- Describe your boat (its type, size, make, color, trim).
- Ask what channel you should change to for their response. Once again, from experience, they will ask you to switch to another channel so channel 16 can be left clear for others to use, should they be in distress.

It goes without saying that you don't want to transmit a distress call unless something serious has happened.

Over the years, the use of cell and smart phones have become increasingly important. Most recently when we contacted the US Coast Guard, they had us switch immediately to our cell phone, and we conducted business with them in that way. Cell phones are also handy when making marina or dinner reservations, checking in with family, and letting people at work or at home know about plan changes. Depending on what kinds of aps you have on your smart phone, you can check email and access the Internet.

However, phones need to be recharged from time to time using 120-volt AC power, and the boat's battery functions with a 12-volt DC battery. In order to solve this dilemma, you need to install a cigarette-lighter socket, if your boat doesn't have one, and plug into it an inverter that changes the battery's 12-volt DC power to 120-volt AC power. Then you can plug in your cell phone and recharge it.

Personal computers (small laptops and notebooks are best for a boat) can also be handy on board, and you can recharge their batteries using an inverter. You can use word processing software to keep your log or diary and download and use software for tide and currents, sailing advice, etc. It would be wise to use surge protectors and to keep the laptop in a dry place away from vibrations. If in port where WiFi is available or if you install a satellite dish, you can access the Internet which has fabulous satellite charts and all sorts of resources.

Nooks, Kindles, and iPads for reading electronic books and iPods or other MP3 players for listening to music are particularly helpful, especially on long cruises. They also can be recharged.

Most people now use Global Positioning System (GPS) devices. This technology depends on earth-orbiting satellites to accurately provide positions to the users. Later versions used mapping technology that let you visually follow your progress on colorful charts. This is extremely helpful in fog or for corroborating sightings which often look very different from their chart representations. For example, once we were in Vinalhaven Island in Penobscot Bay looking for the mouth of a cove where we wanted to anchor. We were heading for an opening in the forest, but noticed that the GPS map marked this as a rock-infested separation rather than the cove opening. We were able to change course in time and find the actual opening and anchor safely. I hate to think of what would have happened if we had pressed through the first gap we spied.

Photo 4:1 Chartplotter from GPS and Radar
Inside the companionway, Tom built a wooden holder for the radar
(in this picture, on the top) and the chartplotter-GPS. A second
GPS with an additional depth sounder is located at the binnacle.

Keeping up with technology and how it changes is just one example of how sailing is a never-ending opportunity to learn something new. Some might throw their hands up in the air and complain, but I think this should be embraced rather than resented. It really is part of the sailing-is-fun principle.

Another principle concerns team work. I learned to sail in team mode so it is the only way I know. I suspect sailing solo has its own set of rules. However, when there is another person on board, people must work together if they are to succeed. What this means is that a person must be aware of what the other is doing and help them meet their objectives while completing their own task at the same time.

For example, let us say that Tom is on the wheel, and I am taking care of the sails. We are on a close reach (sailing with the wind well forward of the beam, but not close-hauled (sailing into the wind)) with the wind coming from the port side, and the genoa off the starboard side of the bow. Tom calls we are going to come about. We are going to change course by heading up into the wind until the sail swings across the bow of the boat to the port side. We will then pull the sail taut while the mainsail flips itself to the other side.

Tom first falls off the wind to achieve the maximum amount of speed that he can. At the same time I wrap the genoa sheet loosely on the winch of the port side of the boat in preparation for pulling it in. When I am ready, Tom turns the boat sharply into the wind. I wait until I see the genoa flapping at the bow of the boat and until the wind starts to push the sail to the port side of the bow. I quickly release the sheet from the starboard-side winch and put another wrap on the port-side winch, pull it in, and wrap it. Because we are on a close reach, Tom might assist me by holding the boat up into the wind for as long as he can without losing speed. That way, the genoa stays loose, allowing me to pull it in quite tightly. Then he falls off to which ever course he planned. All of this happens faster than it takes to explain it, and we never say a word.

Successfully tacking implies that Tom is watching everything I do, and I him, while we both, in a kind of intuitive *pas-de-deux*, help each other out. A lack of coordinated team work makes sailing very difficult if not impossible. This important aspect of the sport was brought home to Tom and me recently when he took a friend and his son out sailing one afternoon. When Tom got home I asked how things had gone. He shook his head and said that they'd had a lot of fun, but it had been a bit difficult because the guests hadn't known what to do. Working as a team on a boat takes time to learn.

A last principle is that on the boat, tasks should be as gender neutral as possible. I am aware that I am entering into dangerous ground here, but this is true for Tom and me, although others might prefer a division of labor based on gender. For us, both men and women ideally need to be able to do anything. It is true that over the years Tom tends to be at the wheel when we dock the boat, and I am at the wheel when we sail through dense fields of lobster pots. But I can dock if I need to, and Tom can of course ably steer us through lobster pots. The same goes for inside the boat. We have refused to identify cooking and washing dishes as woman's work so Tom is as good of a cook as I am, and we both clean up after we eat.

Some couples institute a strict division of labor by sex on the boat. I have sailed with people who allow women only to cook and clean, while men do all the sailing tasks. Every time I tried to pull on a sheet or take my turn on the wheel, the man jumped up and intercepted me. The kitchen was my domain, and he made clear that his wife and I would be doing the cooking and cleaning.

I didn't enjoy that passage. Frankly I was bored and didn't have a good time. Furthermore, the division of labor by sex violated Tom's redundancy-sailing-principle. You may recall that when I met Tom he had already had many sailing experiences. When we first talked about these experiences, he told me that it is vital to have back-up systems in place on board. If the steering wheel cables fail, there is a manual way to steer the boat. If the engine fails, depend on the sails. There are two anchors, two two-way radios, two ways to empty the bilge should we take on water, two GPSs, and two bearing compasses. And so on. Having two people, a man and a woman, who know how to handle the boat is consistent with this principle. If someone gets seriously ill, then the other is competent to work the radio, or if someone goes overboard, then the other knows how to drop the sails and motor back to pick up the person. This is just common sense to us.

My only exception to this rule has to do with the motor. Frankly I can turn it on and off, and that is about it. And I have nightmares about this. My favorite one is that I'm on the boat, and the engine is broken, so I keep stuffing bananas into it. I think this dreams says it all. However, having said that, sailing has taught me more about engines than I would ever have imagined. I have learned where the engine is located (under the companionway stairs); that the boat engine, like a car engine, needs fuel (but of the diesel variety rather than gasoline); that the engine has a transmission (that can fail as it did in Maine one year); that it ultimately rotates the shaft and propeller (which can become tangled up by lobster pot lines, thus stalling the engine); that it can become overheated (when the raw-water-intake valve filter getting clogged with junk), and that if everything functions properly, then maybe, just maybe, the boat goes. Or not. I have more to learn.

SIDE BAR 4:4 THE DINGHY

Dinghies are an important part of the cruising life-style. We have had several different kinds throughout the years we've been sailing. One was hard fiberglass, seven feet in length, which Tom and sometimes I rowed. Our latest one is a rubber, inflatable Zodiac that is ten feet in length that can carry four passengers. We had various boats in between, but this last Zodiac has suited us very well.

Tom resisted buying an outboard motor for the dinghy at first. Being a hard-core Yankee, he wanted to row the little boat. But as our cruising took us further from our home port to distant anchorages and marinas, having an outboard motor on a small dinghy made more and more sense because it would allow us to explore hidden coves and travel more comfortably for longer distances to and from docks. For example, in Ebenecook, a harbor we have frequented for twenty years, the moorings are set some distance from the dock and marina. For Tom to row us to and from the dock several times a day would be arduous.

Our first motor was a two-horse-power outboard engine. After having problems with it constantly overheating, we purchased a second one and got into the habit of having it winterized each year when we took the boat and the dinghy out of the water for winter storage. We never had any problems with it after that.

The outboard motor runs on gasoline, and we have a small gas container that we use to fill up the motor's gas tank. This gas container is stored in an outside compartment safely away from everything. Tom is always very good about making sure the engine has gas, so we never run out of fuel at an inconvenient moment.

Whenever we use the dinghy, I put on my life preserver, and we encourage any passengers to do the same, unless they were children. Then we insist they do so. Tom and I also carry a small dinghy anchor which we use a great deal when we go exploring. We secure the boat by anchoring the anchor in the sand or tying the line to a tree or rock. We also purchased a small pump which we use to remove rain water from the bottom of the boat so our shoes won't get wet. A second pump inflates the dinghy, should it deflate for some reason while we are on land. A strong flashlight for travel by night is important. We use it to alert others to our presence. Oars came with the inflatable, and we sometimes use them if the water is very shallow, and we are afraid that the motor might hit the bottom. We always have the oars in the boat and available in case the motor fails. The anchor, light, and pumps are stored in a canvas bag that we keep in the aft cabin. Whenever we use the dinghy we just grabbed the bag and fling it into the boat, and away we ago.

When leaving the boat or the dock, it is advisable to make sure that the dinghy motor is engaged and running smoothly, so that you don't run into a difficult situation. When arriving at the boat or the dock, a routine should be worked out by the sailors about who is responsible for the painter (the dinghy's bow line). Tom and my routine was the first person on the ladder and into the cockpit carries the painter and cleats it off so that it is secured to the boat. The same went for the dock. The other person follows, carrying any other gear or bags.

Once on cruise up in Maine, we forgot our rule, and neither of us tied off the painter to *Makai*. We had visited Prout's Neck, where at the time Winslow Homer's (1836-1910) painting studio was located. We were sitting in the cockpit having lunch when we saw, about twenty feet from our sailboat, our dinghy bobbing in the water. We scrambled to turn on *Makai's* engine and gently eased over to grab the dinghy's bow line with our pick-pole. Luckily there weren't high seas or strong winds that day.

Arriving at dinghy docks these days and finding a space to tie up your dingy is not easy. At times I have found myself stretched across three boats, grabbing for the dock in order to pull us in. Be prepared to do battle when you arrive at an inflatable dinghy dock.

Dinghy docks can be quite crowded, requiring sailors to be agile and inventive when trying to find a spot.

Photo SB 4:4:1 Dinghy Dock

At the end of each season, besides having the dinghy engine winterized and stored properly, Tom and I lift the dinghy out of the water and transport it home where we thoroughly scrub it down with brushes in the back yard and dry it off before taking out the removable floor boards, deflating the boat, and rolling it up for storage in the dry loft of our garage.

When thinking about what to bring on a boat for a passage, it pays to think about attitude. The principles I have outlined above will go a long way toward helping people maintain their sanity during long periods of living in close, cramped quarters. But more importantly, they will ensure that the responsibilities on board will be comfortably shared and that the crew will be safe. And, of course, the sailing experience will be more fun too.

Tangibles

Probably less important are the tangibles one brings on board. I can make a few observations that might be helpful as you pack your bags for a cruise. Because space is at a premium on board, only pack the essentials. This is also in keeping with the Zen philosophy. Less is definitely better.

To sail comfortably off the coast of New England, even in the summer months, planning is important because, frankly, it is cold and damp. I have found that layers work best. I wear a cotton tee-shirt, a long-sleeved shirt, a sweater (cotton if it is relatively warm and wool for the really cold days with biting winds), and an over-jacket (water repellent). I usually stock multiple tee-shirts, a couple of long-sleeved shirts, and a three pairs of jeans. Denim really stands up to the rigors of life on board. Kneeling on deck, stooping, and bending take their toll. Plus denim is relatively warm. I bring three pairs because if one gets wet, it is good to have a couple of spares. I also pack a couple of pairs of silk long underwear to wear under everything on super-cold days and to wear around the cabin at night under a warm night shirt.

At the wheel, I am frequently exposed to chilly winds. A warm scarf, hat, and sailing gloves are invaluable. The jacket mentioned above is really important. Something both warm and resistant to the damp is worth investing in. I also purchased sailing gloves that not only resist getting wet but have leather palms that allow for manipulating the sail sheets. Tom bought a couple of chemical-resistant gloves that were totally water resistant and found them to be dry and warm, even during night sailing.

For going on land in New England I don't bother to pack a skirt or dress. Rather I bring a nice blouse or light jacket, and some costume jewelry to "dress up" for dinner out. Tom packs a couple of collared shirts and a pair of chinos. He doesn't bring a blazer or a tie. While on a cruise we do not frequent fine-dining restaurants that might require suit jackets and ties for men and dresses for women. In fact, in the small coastal towns and villages that dot the shores of New England, it is rare to find "fancy" restaurants. The one exception is Portland, Maine which is a bona vide city. At the end of our cruises, we usually stay in a yacht club on the south side of the town for a night or two. However, even there, we tend to gravitate to small, unpretentious establishments where sailors in their jeans and fishermen sweaters are not out of place.

Once we stopped in Portland when a cold rain refused to let up. We were on a mooring south of the city, and through the rain and mist we could just make out the lights of downtown Portland. We decided this was not the night to try to go into town. So we used the dinghy to motor to the nearby dock and walked down a street where we stumbled on an old-fashioned pub. This is one of the joys of sailing. You really don't know what treasures await you around the next bend. We went inside and warmed ourselves over hot drinks and hearty pub food. The windows of the establishment looked out on the rain-drenched port and the dim outline of the city. As we savored our meal, we looked around and noticed everyone in the place was wearing the sailor's uniform of jeans, sweaters, boat shoes, and wool jackets. We felt quite at home.

Photo 4:2 Debra in Pub
Pubs and restaurants are readily available at marinas and docks
where sailboats and powerboats dock or grab a mooring ball.

Sailing has required me to pay special attention to my shoes. Some sailors, especially in warmer climates, go barefoot. During one unpleasant heat wave in New Hampshire, where Tom and I don't have air conditioning, we fled to the boat in Pepperrell Cove to find it was stifling even there on the water, and the gnats and mosquitoes tormented us. We set sail for the Isles of Shoals and found a mooring where we spent several days waiting for the heat wave to pass. We were surprised to see another boat from Annapolis, Maryland join us. They were definitely far from their home port. We were interested to see that the couple ran around on board with no shoes, no doubt more of a southern tradition.

I don't dare to do this myself. It is too easy to bump a toe or even cut one's foot while hurrying to set a sail. When speed is of essence it is important to know one's body is well protected. I wear deck shoes or boat shoes that have a non-skid sole. The soles are broken up into many horizontal slits that open and prevent skidding when weight is applied to them. Hard-core sailors recommend using such shoes only on board, worrying that the slits will become damaged and less effective if used extensively on land. Another caveat – boat shoes made of leather are a mixed blessing. Leather is strong and protective, but when wet, especially with salt water, it takes seven days to dry (or at least that is what a sailor told me).

Deck shoes come in a variety of styles. You can buy moccasins, sneakers, or oxford styles. Moccasins are great when it is warm. You can slip them on when you go forward to do something with the anchor locker and kick them off when you settle down to relax in the cockpit. However, they do not support the ankles or the arches. I also bring a pair of regular sneakers for walking on land.

A set of foul-weather gear is vital for sailing comfortably in New England. On a rainy day when it is impossible to lay over and wait for the weather to clear, such gear can be invaluable. It must be both waterproof and breathable. My first set of gear was rubbery which prevented the material from breathing. I found I perspired in it even when I was very chilly, which obviously made me even colder. The gear I use today is made up of breathable 100% water- and wind-proof nylon fabric. It has a brightly-colored jacket with a tight-fitting hood, high collar, lots of pockets that can be closed with Velcro, and a strong zipper. It also has a set of overalls made of the same material. The knees and seat are reinforced for kneeling on deck and long hours of sitting. I also use sailing boots and a rain hat that covers the back of the neck for when the wind and rain are coming from behind.

Photo 4:3 Foul weather gear with Debra at helm.
Foul weather gear is indispensable when sailing. It keeps the sailor warm and dry. It is usually bright yellow as a precaution so that if someone goes overboard, they can be more easily spotted.
Also note that, in front of the wheel at the binnacle,
a second GPS is located for navigation.

Tom and I carry our gear on board in duffle bags rather than suitcases. These soft containers can either be thrown on the aft bunk where they can be easily reached or emptied and stuffed in a drawer until a trip is over. A lot of times I do not unpack but just leave the bag open in the aft cabin where I easily grab what I need. This is sometimes simpler than hanging things up in the lockers or stashing them in drawers. Tom, on the other hand, uses the locker and drawers in the forward cabin where we sleep. He stores everything neatly in its place because, when underway, the boat pitches and rolls, causing everything that is not battened down to fly around.

A small aside – everything-in-its-place can mean things-get-forgotten. Once when we finished up a cruise, I bundled up dirty linen, towels, and clothes. I systematically went through all of the drawers and lockers, and stumbled on a drawer filled with neatly-folded, clean, collared shirts. Tom had placed them in there at the beginning of the cruise and forgotten all about them.

Less-is-better, layers, simplicity, multi-purposed items – all are good principles to remember when packing for a cruise. It is true that space on board is limited, but it is also true that you need to be comfortable and dry while under way. It is a good idea to remember both of these realities and plan accordingly.

Chapter Five

The Southwestern Coast of Maine: Learning the Basics About Sailing

In my early years of summer sailing on *Trull II* and *Northstar,* Tom and I spent every weekend sailing off the southwestern coast of Maine. We drove from Keene in New Hampshire to Kittery Point, Maine on Friday in the late afternoon and returned Sunday night, refreshed and clear-headed in time for work on Monday morning. The area I talk about in this chapter stretches from Kittery and Portsmouth Harbor (see 70.704 west longitude 43.077 north latitude and then pan northeast, past York, Cape Neddick, Ogunquit, Perkins Cove, Wells, Kennebunkport, and, finally, on to Cape Porpoise with Stage Harbor on its north side, ending at 70.422 west longitude 43.367 north latitude). For several years we sailed up and down this part of the coast, visiting some of these towns or just watching them go by as we sailed along. I consider this part of Maine to be where I did my basic training.

Southwestern Maine is different from eastern Maine in that the coastline is less craggy and tough. Instead of rocks and ever-green forests defining the shores as they do up in Muscongus Bay, the soft beaches and dunes of Ogunquit and Wells gently meet the waves. Tourists have eagerly moved into this part of Maine in the summer, enjoying the seaside villages, harbors, and bays. Motels, hotels, and summer cottages line the beaches of Kennebunkport, Wells, and York, welcoming those who share an enthusiasm for Maine's attractions. Amidst the excited throngs, Tom and I headed for the boat in Pepperrell Cove, where all we heard were the cries of the herring and black-back gulls and the sound of halyards singing against the boats' masts around us.

SIDE BAR 5:1 SAILS AND THEIR USES

In order to understand sails, it is important to know the names of the points of the sail. Triangular sails have three points: the lower front point (tack), the top point (head) and the aft point (clew).

The mainsail attaches to the mast and the boom. Both the mast and the boom have tracks along which the slides for the mainsail move. When the sail is attached, the slides between the tack and the clew are stretched along the boom by the outhaul. This is a rope or cable that runs through the boom, over a pulley and to the clew of the main. The clew is permanently secured in this taut position. As the head is hoisted (raised) by the main halyard, the slides along the forward edge of the sail glide up the mast. Once the halyard is tightly secured, the sail becomes closely bonded to the mast, inhibiting openings for wind to escape and ensuring a smooth foil (curve of the sail) to develop when sailing.

On keelboats such as *Northstar* and *Makai*, the mainsail is attached to the boom and mast at the beginning of the season and left that way, being wrapped and stored under a cover on top of the boom when not in use. On smaller sailboats, sailors have to rig (attach) the mainsail each time they go sailing.

When the mainsail is hoisted in preparation for going sailing, the boat must be turned into the wind (face the wind). That way, the mainsail does not fill with wind; it just flaps around. Once hoisted, the mainsheet (line that controls the boom and, consequently, the mainsail) is the primary means for trimming the mainsail. As you turn the boat with the tiller or the wheel so that the wind is, for example, on the beam, you can pull in the mainsheet until the sail fills. Then the boat will begin to move forward.

The storm jib is a small sail made of heavy material. Its purpose is to help keep the boat pointed into the wind in heavy weather. The tack of the storm jib secures to the bow of the boat. Its head is raised by the forward halyard, or, in the case of roller reefing/furling, by a separate halyard. Its clew is secured to the two main sheets attached to the main winches normally servicing the working jib. If you have roller furling/reefing, do not assume that a small amount of sail from that system will act as a storm jib! It is too high up. Fully furl your sail and secure it with straps. Then deploy your legitimate storm jib.

The working jib is the workhorse of the sails which when combined with the main is the normal configuration for sailing. If conditions warrant, it can be combined with the jigger (aft sail on a yawl) for long hauls without the mainsail. This is an excellent configuration for night sailing in strong winds. Tom told me he once used this configuration to sail from Canaveral Florida to Bermuda on the same tack in little over six days.

The larger jibs (125%, and 150%) are progressively lighter sails. The "%" designation refers to the distance from the bow of the boat to the mast. This means that the 150% genoa has a lower edge that is one and a half times the length of the measurement from the bow of the boat to the mast. These sails are used with increasingly light winds.

The drifter is a large sail made from lightweight material. It is used in very light winds, and its sheets are secured to blocks far aft on the boat. This sail is somewhat new, and it seems to have replaced the spinnaker on pleasure boats.

The spinnaker is a special breed of sail. It is a large sail made of light material for use in light winds which are blowing on the stern quarters of the boat. The spinnaker flies high up in front of the boat. It is an equilateral triangle with a belly. On the front of the mast is a slotted channel. Attached to this channel is the spinnaker bell, a rounded tube into which the spinnaker pole inserts. The spinnaker pole has clip eyes on its ends. This allows it to attach to the bell and to the sail. The head (top) of the sail is hoisted by the main halyard. The spinnaker pole is attached to one of the corners with the guy (a rope running to the main winch on that side of the boat), and the sheet (rope) is attached to the main winch on the other side of the boat. For example, if the spinnaker is flying on the starboard side of the boat, the spinnaker pole and guy would be attached to the left clew of the sail. The guy would then run through the port side block to the port winch. The sheet would run through the starboard block to the starboard winch. (See Figure 5:1 Sail Configurations for a Sloop.) If the spinnaker is on the port side, everything reverses. The spinnaker pole and guy change to the right hand clew, and the sheet attaches to the left clew. Actually the ropes stay put with changed names, and the pole is switched from one clew to the other which can be an exciting maneuver.

Figure SB 5:1 Sail Configurations for a Sloop.

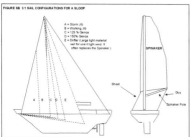

On keelboats such as *Northstar* and *Makai*, the foresail was hoisted at the beginning of the season and left that way, rolled up on a roller-furling forestay. On smaller boats like *Trull II,* Tom had to rig the foresail each time we went sailing. Furling lines attached to it are pulled aft to the cockpit on each side of the boat and secured there. When you want to use the foresail, you pull on the furling line on the side of the boat (starboard or port) where you want the foresail. The line turns the drum of the roller-furling mechanism, unwinding the foresail. This same line will allow you to pull the foresail in tight (if you are close-hauled for example) or let it out loosely (if the wind is behind you). Winches on either side of the cockpit provide mechanical advantage so that the foresaid is more easily managed. Wrap the line around the winch in a clockwise direction one to three times and pull it (it will only turn clockwise). If you need additional force, insert the winch handle and grind (turn it). A second person can tail the line (pull on the line while you crank the winch), which makes the grinding more effective.

Southwestern Maine was a good place for me to begin to learn the "ABCs" of what sailing is all about. And one of the first lessons Tom taught me was the difference between *running, reaching,* and *beating.* He did this on afternoon sails out to the Isles of Shoals, the group of granite islands off the coast of New Hampshire. Going back and forth to these islands gave me ample opportunities for learning how to trim the sails when the wind was behind us, on our beam (on our side), or coming across the bow. Generally we would run before the wind going out to the Isles and sail back on a reach or beating with the wind on our side or from in front of the boat. Besides providing my training ground for sailing, these trips gave us a chance to explore the islands.

SIDE BAR 5:2 TRIMMING THE SAIL AND RUNNING, REACHING, AND BEATING

When Tom first tried to teach me about sails, he described two different concepts: heading up (turning the boat into the wind) and bearing away (turning the boat away from the wind). These two ideas are important for understanding how to optimally use a sail; that is, how to properly trim a sail.

For example, let's say you have the mainsail hoisted, and the wind is on the beam. If you begin to head up, then the mainsail will begin to luff (flutter) a little, and the boat's speed will slacken. If you bear away, then it will tautly fill with wind again, and the boat's speed will increase. You can achieve the same effects if you release the mainsheet a little (the mainsail luffs) and if you pull it in (the mainsail is full). It is possible to over-trim a sail. When you do this, then the boat's speed will also begin to drop. A properly-trimmed sail is almost a work-of-art and can only be achieved with experience and experimentation on the part of the sailor.

The trim of a foresail is also important. After you pull out the genoa, for example, it will flap in the wind. Begin to adjust its position by pulling on the sheet. Use the winches and winch handle if necessary. (See Side Bar 5:1.) As you pull in the sheet, watch for the luffing to cease. If you have pulled the sheet in too far, then the mainsail will begin to luff. The two sails are trying to do two different things. The mainsail is trying to push/pull the boat into the wind, while the foresail is pulling the boat off the wind. It's the sailor's job to balance them, and when they are, neither is luffing. With two sails up, you will notice a difference in the boat's speed and maneuverability because the wind is flowing correctly through the slot between the two sails, creating the ideal aerodynamic shapes. The sum of their power is greater than the two parts because both boost the flow of air over the other in a synergistic fashion (ASA 2010, p. 44).

Telltales, made of pieces of colored cloth, show sailors that their foresail is trimmed optimally. Telltales are sewn on the foresail about a foot from the forestay on both sides of the sail. When the sail is trimmed properly, then both of the telltales fly straight back. If the sail is over-trimmed, then the telltale on the leeward side of the foresail flies up, and if the sail is under-trimmed, then the telltale on the windward side rises. Mainsails may also have telltales but they are not as helpful.

If the boat comes to a stop with its bow heading up into the wind, and it is unresponsive to the tiller or the wheel, then sailors say that it is "in irons." This sometimes happens to us when there is a very light wind because *Makai* responds best to a robust breeze. When in irons, release the mainsheet so that the mainsail is free, and then turn the wheel or push the tiller to one side of the boat or the other. After a while, the wind will push the boat backwards and cause it to turn. Keep the wheel turned until the wind is coming on the side of the boat, or at least solidly in one of the bow quarters. Then trim the mainsail and turn the wheel in the direction you want it go.

Running, reaching, and *beating* are three concepts that are fundamental to sailing. *Running* is sailing with the wind behind you. The wind comes over the stern and fills the sails, pushing the boat along. The mainsail and/or the genoa can be in play, depending on the wind and the captain's evaluation. With the wind behind the boat, it is usually not as chilly as it is when the breeze comes across the bow. While it is great to have a warm sail, sometimes the seas build, and the boat surfs along in front of them which can be uncomfortable after a while.

On a *reach* the wind comes across the boat perpendicularly. A *broad reach* is when the angle of the wind to the boat is between about 150 and 110 degrees, a *beam reach* is when it is between 70 and 110 degrees, and a *close reach* is when the angle is about 40 to 70 degrees. Anything smaller than 40 degrees is *beating. Beating* (sailing close-hauled) is sailing as closely into the wind as possible. This is when the sails are pulled in quite flat and taut.

It is easy to understand how the wind fills the sail when the boat is running. However, it is not so obvious when the boat is beating, and the Bernoulli Principle is in operation. This principle works with airplanes and with sails. When wind passes over a sail or wing, a vacuum is created on the windward side. This vacuum pulls the boat into it. It took me a quite a while to puzzle through this dynamic and to understand that pulling a sail back tautly during beating or on a close reach is actually creating a vacuum that the boat is sucked into.

The Isles of Shoals are a truly amazing place (see 70.613 west longitude 42.982 north latitude). They are a strange mixture of rocky austerity and cultural richness. On them you can find evidence of Captain John Smith visiting in the 1500s, when only Native Americans fished there, and Celia Leighton Thaxter living comfortably in the 1800s where she tended a garden that has been restored for people to visit. Thaxter, born in Portsmouth, New Hampshire, not only lived on the Isles where her father managed a hotel during that period, but she also created a summer Mecca for artists such as Frederick Childe Hassam (1859-1935), the late-nineteenth-century American Impressionist painter.

I have many wonderful memories of sitting out in the cockpit, with the boat moored in the waters between Star and Smuttynose Islands. Gosport Harbor, the Isles main harbor, was created by the construction of breakwaters that join the islands of Star, Cedar, Smuttynose, and Malaga. It is sheltered to a certain extent, although frankly, I seem to remember all too often lying in my bunk and hearing the howl of the winds and the crash of the waves as they pushed into the harbor. North of the port and the main islands lies Duck Island that is covered with bird guano. You don't have to get too close to this place to smell its pungent odor. White Island lies to the south, where a 82-foot lighthouse marks the treacherous rocky ledges that surround the islands.

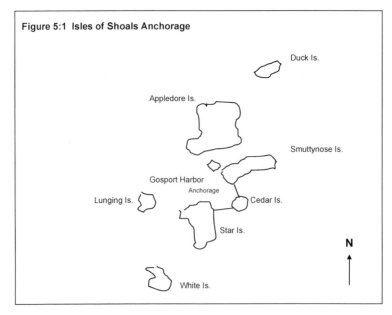

Figure 5:1 Isles of Shoals Anchorage

Photo 5:1 Isles of Shoals Stone Church
The stone Gosport Chapel is one of Star Island's prominent
features. Sometimes, at the close of the day, Shoalers gather together
with lighted candles and walk up the hill to the chapel.

There is much to see and do on the Isles of Shoals. First we explored
Star Island. We motored by dingy over to the dock used by the *Thomas
Leighton* ferry that runs between Portsmouth and the Isles of Shoals. We
walked up to the large white conference center where a huge verandah
wraps around the lobby. We also visited the stone village where there is
a library, a church and other cottages. Star Island has some wonderful
trails that take you to the far reaches of the island, allowing for the
observation of the bird colonies and the ever-restless sea.

East of Star Island is tiny Cedar Island where a lobster man and his
family used to live in a small house. He was a real entrepreneur who
sold huge lobster rolls to boaters who came to his dock and waved to

him or his wife. A couple of times during the summer we ordered these sumptuous sandwiches, eating them in the cockpit of the boat as the gulls swirled overhead waiting for treats. Each time we swore we'd never had a better-tasting lobster roll anywhere.

North of Cedar is Smuttynose Island where we discovered a small cottage, a graveyard, and more bird colonies. Herring and black-back gulls dominate, but there are also sleek black cormorants drying their feathers on the rocks near the shore. Attached to Smuttynose is the small island of Malaga where we once found an archaeological field school in progress. The director was there, and he told us about the Native American site that he had uncovered. Apparently for hundreds of years, perhaps even thousands, before Europeans came, Native Americans fished from the Isles of Shoals.

Northwest of Smuttynose is a narrow gut that separates it from Appledore Island. Sometimes, when we don't want to stop for a lobster roll or to spend the night, we sail around the back north side of Appledore and south, down through the gut which divides the two islands. Houses which are part of a marine station line it. Appledore is the largest of the islands, and we have spent many afternoons exploring this interesting place. The Shoals Marine Laboratory is located there, as is Thaxter's restored garden.

York Harbor, already mentioned in Chapter 2, is also nearby, yet far enough to provide learning opportunities. Made up of a number of individual communities such as York Village, York Beach, York Harbor, and Cape Neddick, it has a fascinating history that includes Abenaki (Native American group) raids, English Loyalists, and shipbuilding in the 1800s. In the center of York Village, there are many beautiful buildings and homes. It was easy to sail in, pick up a mooring, and walk into town. One year we were on the Pepperrell Cove Yacht Club Great Race Committee. The Committee organized an afternoon race which ended in York Harbor with dinner at a local restaurant and mock prizes and hilarious speeches. Later that evening there were reports of attacks made by would-be pirates who carried squirt guns and water-filled balloons. They were accompanied by hoots of laughter.

Further north along the coast is Cape Neddick where Nubble lighthouse attracts tourists and artists who come to photograph or paint it. This quintessential Maine icon is bright white and red and stands 88 feet above the ground. Even when you are quite far out to sea, you can see it on the coast or hear its horn. Once we anchored in Cape Neddick Harbor, northeast of Nubble, just beyond Short Sands Beach. If you look at the charts, they indicate that there is an anchorage area in the northern corner of the bay. If the seas are coming from the southeast, or even the east, there's not a lot of protection. The time we stayed there, it was foggy with no wind or seas to speak of, so our stay there was calm. Nonetheless, it was eerie hearing the fog horn all night. I remember that we didn't sit out that night, partially because of the clammy dampness of the fog, but also because of the spooky atmosphere created by the fog horn and the bats that flew around the lighthouse.

That evening, we listened to "The Fog Horn" which is a story written by the science-fiction writer Ray Bradbury. It's a poignant story about the sound of a lighthouse's fog horn attracting the attention of a primordial sea monster who amorously comes to court the tower, but ends up destroying it when it realizes the lighthouse is not responding to its advances. It was not exactly a good idea to listen to this story when we were near a lighthouse like Nubble on a night when we couldn't see a foot in front of us.

Tiny Perkins Cove, a harbor with a village that caters to tourists, and popular Ogunquit are located northeast of Cape Neddick and Nubble Light. We have never sailed into Perkins Harbor because it is too small and crowded to accommodate a sailboat of our size. But we have driven there to see the shops and restaurants which are a lot of fun.

Kennebunkport is an old prestigious town in which the President George Herbert Bush and his wife have a summer home. Once we motored up the narrow, shallow Kennebunk River and secured transient dock space at a local marina. Then we walked around the town admiring the old homes and visiting shops. I remember we ate on board that night and walked into town again later and had ice cream. The sidewalks were packed with people, and I sensed a holiday, carnival atmosphere.

By the time Tom and I began to visit Cape Porpoise in *Northstar*, I felt we were very intrepid indeed. Cape Porpoise was about five or six hours from our mooring in Pepperrell Cove and involved us spending the night before coming home. However, it was not convenient for sailors to stop there because it was a working harbor, and lobster boats and pots crowded into it. Also there were no services for sailors. None-the-less we have sailed into Cape Porpoise several times and dropped an anchor. Once we sailed there with some friends and were attacked by small biting flies around Boone Island which is notorious for being where a ship crashed in the worst of winter. Those who survived did so only by practicing cannibalism.

Another time I remember that we stopped at Cape Porpoise and went in to the small village to walk around. We had a drink in a pub as the sun set and then returned to the boat. The wind picked up during the night, and the next morning we faced seas and brisk winds on our way back to Pepperrell Cove. Tom decided that this would be a good opportunity to formally introduce me to the concepts of *coming about* and *tacking*. Up to this point I had been more-or-less following his directions when we were on a reach or beating. I moved the genoa from one side of the boat to the other, as the boat changed course, whenever he told me. But now he wanted me to be more aware of what I was doing. Coming about is changing tack. I asked Tom about the difference between tacking and jibing. Tom explained that you jibe when you are running before the wind and want to change direction, while when you come about, the wind is on the bow or side of the boat. With these key concepts under my belt I felt that I had taken a big step because they are some of the basic principles of sailing.

SIDE BAR 5:3 TACKING, COMING ABOUT, AND JIBING

Tacking occurs when the boat is moving against the wind. Because you can't sail directly into the wind, you steer the boat slightly to one side, and then on the other, from which the wind is coming. Going through a series of maneuvers that resemble a zigzag brings the boat gradually closer to your destination. It is this zigzag effect that tacking produces.

Tom instructed me to "think of zigzagging along a line." Each of the zigzags would be about 45 degrees from the direct line you are hoping to travel. He told me to think of the wind coming from one direction and then the other, and of moving the boat first to the right and then to the left of the line. When I first learned about this maneuver, I wished that the wind were not so strong. But as I practiced tacking, I noticed that the strength of the wind allowed me to come about (change tack) more easily than I could have if the wind had been light.

We were spending the night in Stage Harbor, and Pepperrell Cove lay southwest from us. After leaving Stage Horbor and going to the whistle that lay about a mile and a half from the entrance, I sailed to the starboard side of the course line and set the sails as tightly as possible. Then I headed up into the wind, watching the sails until they started to luff, at which point I adjusted my course by falling off the wind. I sailed to the port side of the course line, and again positioned the sails as tautly as I could. By going back and for this way, I maximized my forward progress. Tom carefully watched my maneuvers, encouraging and critiquing as we went along.

One thing about tacking, which is probably obvious, is that it takes longer to get to where you need to go than if you motor directly to your destination. As we traveled home from Cape Porpoise, the afternoon slowly wore on. First I went in one direction, away from the land; then in the other direction, closer to the coast. I felt we were inching slowly toward the Whaleback lighthouse which marks the opening of Portsmouth Harbor. But as the hours passed I forgot about how slowly we were moving toward our destination and took pleasure in the way that *Northstar* responded to the wind as we sailed along the coast. And because I had to think about where we were going and to strategize how to get there, I had a different perspective than if I had just been relaxing in the cockpit or even moving the genoa back and forth when Tom told me.

In a controlled jibe, the stern of the boat passes through the direction of the wind, and the boom flips to the opposite side of the boat. In preparing for this maneuver, it is essential to first release the preventer, then to rapidly pull in on the main halyard, and when the boom approaches the midpoint of the boat, secure the halyard. Once the boom flips to the opposite side, release the main halyard, and allow the boom to move to its new position. Secure the main halyard, and reposition the preventer to the boom in the new location. (Tip: It is essential to secure the boom tightly when it flips, because if it were not, then the boom would have altogether too much force and could cause major damage.)

On our way to Pepperrell Cove from Cape Porpoise we passed Wells and Ogunquit, and when we were off of Bald Head Cliff where the Cliff House Hotel is visible from the water on the coast, Tom took over for a while, giving me a break. I stretched and massaged my right arm which was stiff from pushing the tiller. I went below and heated up some minestrone which I brought up into the cockpit in small bowls. I ate mine quickly and took back the tiller so that Tom could eat his before it got cold in the chilly sea air.

SIDE BAR 5:4 PREVENTERS AND CONTROLLED JIBES

The preventer is a very useful piece of equipment. It consists of a length of strong sheet-quality line which runs through two double blocks and is equipped with fittings so that the blocks can quickly be attached to the boom and strong deck fittings. These fittings should be located on the port and starboard rail just fore of the mast and at the bottom center of the boom.

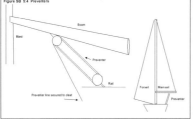

Figure SB 5:4 Preventers

The preventer pulls down and forward on the boom when the boat is on a broad reach or running configuration. It keeps the boom from flying up with the gusts of wind and increases the pulling efficiency of the sail. It also "prevents" an accidental jibe from taking place when the wind is behind you. An accidental jibe is when the wind catches the back of the mainsail and flips it to the opposite side of the boat. This is no big deal as far as the foresails are concerned; however, on a large boat, the rapid redeployment of the mainsail can cause injury to a crew member and/or damage to the boat.

The preventer should be deployed before you assume the running configuration. If the mainsail is positioned off the starboard side of the boat, position the preventer between the starboard deck fitting and the boom. As you let the mainsail out to the running position, tighten the preventer securing the boom in place. If you perform a calculated jibe, pull in on the main sheet as you slacken the preventer. When the boom is over the center of the boat, lock the main sheet in its jaws and allow the boom to snap to the opposite side (a short distance with the main sheet locked and the boom over the center of the boat). Switch the preventer to the port deck fitting and slowly let out on the main sheet and tighten the preventer line until you have the boom in the running position on the port side of the boat.

Using the preventer properly insures that you achieve maximum efficiency from your mainsail and that your sailing experience will be a safe one.

Ahead I saw Nubble light. We were three quarters of the way home. I looked forward to getting to Pepperrell Cove and relaxing before having a nice dinner. We approached Gerrish Island on the north side of Portsmouth Harbor. Off it, Nun '2' marks the treacherous East and West Sisters. We took those rocks seriously and didn't take a shortcut inside Nun '2', but decorously went around it. Back in the 1980s an uninformed powerboat went inside the nun to get into Portsmouth Harbor. The rocks tore the bottom of the boat off, and they took on water rapidly. No lives were lost, but many still talk about the frantic radio calls the owners sent out as their boat began to sink. The lesson to all boaters was sobering.

Northstar glided by '2KR' which marks Kitts Rocks and turned up into the entrance of the harbor. Portsmouth Harbor must be one of the most picturesque places I know. On each side there are sandy beaches interspersed with impressive outcrops. On the north side of the harbor is my all-time favorite lighthouse – the brown-stone Whaleback Lighthouse (the first version built in 1829), and on the south side, on New Castle Island, is the white Portsmouth Harbor Lighthouse which is said to be haunted. Further east are mudflats that the birds love to frequent at low tide.

Photo 5:2 Whaleback Lighthouse
Whaleback Lighthouse is my favorite light. It was first
constructed offshore of Fort Foster and Wood Island, Kittery,
Maine in 1820. It was rebuilt with granite blocks in 1880.

SIDE BAR 5:5 GULLS AND TERNS

While in Pepperrell Cove or when sailing, we see a lot of gulls. Great black-backed gulls are the largest gulls in the United States. They are generally about 30 inches in size, white with black wings and backs, and have yellow bills with a red dot on them and pink legs. The Smithsonian Guide calls them "coastal predators" and says they are proficient at harassing other birds and robbing their nests (Burnie 2012, p. 142). They are frequently found close to human settlements and their refuse dumps. They tend to remain in coastal areas and do not wander inland.

Another common gull we often see is the herring gull which is also large, although not as big as the black-backed gull. It is white with grey, black-tipped wings and has a yellow beak with a red dot on it. Its legs are flesh colored. When they breed in the summer, they do so in colonies. My Audubon field guide notes that they eat fish and shell fish, and there is evidence that they drop the shell fish deliberately on rocks from the air to break them open. Even more so than great black-back gulls, herring gulls are scavengers who frequent dumps. We see them in shopping centers on the New Hampshire coast where they hang out near the dumpsters. The field guide also notes that in many places herring gulls are spreading, possibly because of their scavenging skills, and that they are out-competing smaller birds such as laughing gulls and terns (p. 446).

The cry of the herring gull is distinctive, and I always associate it with the Isles of Shoals, where there are large numbers of them. When Tom and I visited and explored the Isles, it was not difficult to find the nesting areas of black-back and herring gulls. Their raucous cries incessantly filled the air, and the smell of guano was pungent. Light-brown immature gulls, with heads submissively lowered, scurried underfoot, peeping. Picked-over shells and eggs were spread all over the rocks. (Tip: Wear an old hat to protect yourself against the birds' retaliatory droppings.)

At least two different kinds of terns populate Pepperrell Cove. Both have the distinctive tern cap and forked tails. The first is named little tern. These are quite small, 9 inches in size, with yellow bills, white undersides, and gray backs and black-tipped wings. I believe the other terns are common terns. They are larger than the little tern and possess white undersides with dark-tipped gray backs. Their bills are red-orange with a black tip. Common terns have a summer range in our area. Their presence in the Cove is a tribute to the concerted efforts of the NH Fish and Game and the Audubon Society of New Hampshire described in a television program called *Wild Life Journal* which aired on NH public television in 2003. Apparently these birds disappeared from the area 60 years ago, casualties of hunters, hat-makers, and seagull. In 1997 NH Fish and Game and the Audubon Society reintroduced common terns into the Isles of Shoals. Volunteers actually set out painted wooded terns and played CD recordings of tern colonies to attract the birds. (I thought this quite clever, even funny.) Their efforts paid off. Soon the birds were sighted. In the 1980s we hardly ever saw terns, and herring and black-backed gulls dominated the cove. But following these conservation efforts, the terns really invaded Pepperrell Cove. By 2003 they appeared to be in healthy competition with the gulls. By the way, the program mentions that this restoration project was funded in part by the sale of conservation license plates to New Hampshire drivers – perhaps one good reason to purchase one?

As we sailed toward the cove, another sailboat came toward us. I asked Tom if we were going to collide with it because it seemed like we were on the same tack. "Maybe," was his laconic reply. "Look and see if its motor is on," he told me. I did so but saw no water coming out of the exhaust. I believed it was under sail. Tom said that sailboats not motoring have the right of way if they are approaching you from the starboard side. I later looked this up, and the actual rule states that a boat 112.5 degrees or less off the starboard bow has the right of way. However, who is going to quibble when they are out on the water? This boat was approaching us from the starboard, so I gave way.

Tom added that if two boats were on the same tack, then the leeward (on the side away from the wind) boat has priority over the windward boat. That is, the boat on the side from which the winds is blowing should be able to slip behind the other boat if it wants to cross the other boat's path. When I drew a diagram of this later, it made sense to me. The boat on the windward side would have more control over itself than the one on the leeward side; thus the second boat, having less access to the wind, should be given the right of way.

As we passed Whaleback Lighthouse Tom suggested that we turn on the motor and take the sails down before entering the cove. I turned the boat out of the way of the oncoming sailboat as Tom switched on the engine, and I remained at the tiller until he got the sails in. Then I motored over to our mooring where Tom picked up the mooring pole and secured us. It had been quite a day.

During these early days of sailing we did not only go east into Maine. Sometimes we went west and south to Massachusetts, and I learned a lot during those voyages too. One lesson concerned sailing in gusty wind. We were on our way to the Merrimack River and Newburyport in *Northstar*. The wind was on the nose of the boat. With each blast Tom would swing the bow of the boat upwind until the gust diminished. Then he would fall off. If the gust continued for quite some time, he instructed me to loosen the main sheet, so we dropped off the wind to a reach which made for a gentler ride. As I practiced doing this, I realized that sailing is never a static experience. The sailor must always be attuned to the wind, seas, and boat, making adjustments constantly.

Heeling was another lesson. Strong gusts of wind push the boat on its side, but this effect can also be achieved by a sailor pulling the sails in tight when the wind is on the nose. I think there are two kinds of sailors: ones who minimize heeling because of the wear and tear on the boat, and ones who live for heeling and the excitement of "burying the rail" in the water as the boat skims across the surface of the sea. I'm hard to label. It depends on the situation and how I'm feeling. I love the excitement of speed, but I'm also nervous if the wind and waves are so strong that I'm uncertain of what control we have over the boat. As in gusty winds, when you want to reduce heeling, point the boat up into the wind.

Strong winds and rough seas cause difficulties for boaters, as they did on the trip we took to Newburyport one weekend. The wind was irregular with one blast after another, causing us to constantly trim the sails. Plus, the seas were building, and we slammed into them as the afternoon wore on. Around three o'clock the charts alerted us that we were close to the mouth of the Merrimack River. We started toward the mouth of the river but very large seas thrashed us about. Apparently the tide was going out, and the current from the Merrimack River was extraordinarily strong. We loosened the sails and turned on the motor, fighting our way into the river. I had never been in seas like that (this was before I was introduced to the waters between the Kennebec River and Seguin Island in Maine) and found myself thrown from one side of the cockpit to the other. I hung on as hard as I could, but was horrified to see that at times *Northstar* heeled so far over that the side of the boat was in the water. In fact, we were actually taking on water. I nervously asked Tom if everything was all right, and he answered grimly that he hoped so.[1]

---

[1] We visited Newburyport many times. Once we saw a small powerboat drive out toward the mouth of the river, presumably to fish. A short time later, with sirens blaring and blue lights flashing, a harbor police vessel sped by us. They returned with the small powerboat in tow. The rough waters of the Merrimac River's mouth had defeated them. Luckily no lives were lost.

Northstar struggled through the chaotic mouth of the river and slid into the relatively quiet of its upper reaches. Then we motored upstream to the American Yacht Club in Newburyport with which our Pepperrell Cove Yacht Club had a reciprocal agreement at that time. Tom grabbed a mooring, and a friendly launch driver from the club came over and greeted us. He told us a bit about the club and the town, and before he left, he warned us to be careful of using the dinghy when the tide was going out or in. He said that there was a very strong current and to try to move around when the water was slack. He got no argument from us. We waited until evening and then went into the lovely, old, grey-shingled club that had wonderful photographs on the walls that documented the history of the club. In addition Newburyport was undergoing a Renaissance, and there were a lot of new shops and galleries. We stopped at a trendy café for a bite to eat before returning to the boat.

The next morning Tom and I were careful to leave when the tide was slack and passed through the mouth of the river. It was difficult by the standards of Portsmouth Harbor's mouth, but it was bearable, unlike the day before when we actually took on water. As we sailed back home, I realized I had a new appreciation for the power of the wind, currents, and tides.

This chapter describes some of the basic terms and concepts one needs to know about sailing: tacking and coming about, jibing and running before the wind, right of way, heeling, and coping with seas and gusty winds. It is a lot to absorb, and it is only over time with experience that one really comes to understand this information so one can intuitively respond correctly in a crisis.

Chapter Six

Provincetown: My First Big Passage

Tom and I decided to take a trip, referred to as a "passage" by sailors, on *Northstar*. We planned to go to Provincetown, Massachusetts (70.877 west longitude 42.513 north latitude) which is located at the tip of Cape Cod. Since it was before the days of the Loran or GPS systems, we were compelled to spend long hours poring over charts to prepare our course.

SIDE BAR 6:1 CHARTS

Charts are essential tools for navigation. Consider charts to be like maps you use when driving your car. When Tom and I first started traveling from our home port we purchased sets of charts published by the National Oceanographic and Atmospheric Administration (NOAA). We still have these charts, but now we also have electronic charts on our GPS. We rely on both.

Charts are indispensable tools in that they not only mark rocks, ledges, and other obstructions you must avoid, but they also calculate routes for boaters. For example, on the chart for Casco Bay, various distances and routes are calculated for the sailor. From Littlejohn Island to Great Diamond Island, the course of 229 degrees for five miles is marked, and from Whaleboat Island to Peaks Island the course is 243 degrees for 6.4 miles. Various cans, nuns, and whistles allow you to see progress as you sail along.

On the Y axis of the chart, degrees and minutes of latitude are shown, and on the X axis, you see degrees and minutes of longitude. You will also find what is called a compass rose on the chart. It is made up of two concentric circles (roses), the outer one designating true north and the inner one showing magnetic north. Magnetic variation (the difference between true north and magnetic north) is usually printed in the center of the compass rose. The chart before me of Casco Bay indicates the variation is 17 degrees west (for that year and that location). The reason that magnetic north is important is because your boat's compass records magnetic north and not true north. Thus, to calculate accurate routes, you must convert the route to your

---

destination to one consistent with the magnetic north compass. (The sample routes on the NOAA charts take into consideration the magnetic north compass. But if you want to go somewhere for which the NOAA charts don't provide a course, then you must do the math yourself.)

Before GPS, Tom and I charted our own courses using old-fashioned technology such as pencils, dividers, and parallel rulers. We drew a penciled line between where we were and where we wanted to go, lay one edge of the parallel ruler along the line, and "walked" the ruler to where an edge crossed through the center of the compass rose, passing through both the true north and magnetic north compasses. The number of degrees where it crossed the magnetic rose was the new course we would follow that day. Then we used our marine compass which was attached to the helm to determine our route and set our sails.

When planning a passage it is also essential to estimate distance and time between destinations. One nautical mile is the length of one minute of latitude. Unlike longitude which changes depending on where you are on the planet, latitude remains constant and should be used for measuring travel distance. Once again, I can use the chart of Casco Bay that is in front of me. Using dividers, I place one point on the Flashing Gong "3" off of the northeast side of Peaks Island. The chart locates it at 43 degrees 39.8 minutes latitude, 70 degrees 10.1 minutes longitude in a box for the sailor's convenience. I place the other point on the green can "1" off the northeast side of Great Diamond Island. Holding the divider steady, I move the divider points, placing them on the latitude scale conveniently placed on the chart and estimate the number of minutes between the points. This will give you the distance in nautical miles. For this sample trip, the chart estimates it is about one and a half nautical miles. *Makai* travels about five nautical miles an hours, so (1.5 nautical miles X 5 nautical miles per hour = .3 hours or about 18 to 20 minutes). Thus our estimated time of arrival at the green can "1" is about 20 minutes after we take off.

Tom always insists that we keep a careful log of our passages. In these we include the date, time on the water, time under sail, distance traveled, the direction and speed of the wind and currents, and engine hours run. If you have a GPS or a Loran, then make note of your position at each entry. In foggy or dark conditions, entries into the log should take place on the half hour, or at least on the hour. If you lose GPS or Loran power, then you will be able to estimate where you are using the log data. (Tom also checks to see if the bilge pump was working at this juncture by turning the switch to manual for a second, and then back to automatic.)

As time went on our logs have become more like scrap books as we collected information about anchorages, moorings, yacht clubs, marinas, restaurants, post cards, tickets for places we've been, and other helpful observations we've built on over the years. It is a wonderful time, at the end of the day, when we sit in the cockpit, or down in the main cabin if it's raining, and review our day and make note of what we've done.

We planned to sail from Pepperrell Cove, south to Cape Ann. The Annisquam River-Canal flows between Cape Ann and the main land where we would pick up a mooring and spend the night. The next day we'd sail to Salem and arrange for dock space in a marina. On day three of our passage we'd pass Boston Harbor on our way to Scituate. And finally we would sail across Massachusetts Bay to Provincetown. On the return, our plan was to vary our course slightly, stopping at Scituate and Gloucester before sailing back around Cape Ann and heading for our home port. During each sailing day we planned to cover between 20 and 30 miles which we estimated would take at least 5 or more hours.[2] We intended to take lay-over days in Salem, Provincetown and perhaps Gloucester. All of this, of course, was contingent upon good sailing weather, no boat problems, etc. We kept in mind the principle of flexibility.

Since this was my first passage, I didn't fully realize how important this kind of planning is. On any passage, it is vital to decide what your main goal is, then ascertain how far your vessel comfortably goes in a day (in our case, that was about 20 to 30 miles a day of sailing), and choose places to stop along the way. Use charts and books about the region to help you identify anchorages, marinas, and other facilities where you can stop along the way to your destination. If you love nature and quiet, build in more anchorages. If you want an urban experience, seek dock spaces or moorings in marinas or yacht clubs that are in or near cities. Always build in extra days and places for bad weather and/ or boat problems. And remember that you will need to pump out your holding tank, restock the larder, buy diesel, get fresh ice for the ice box, and fill up the water tank occassionally.

Getting over-excited during a cruise and pushing to go further without due planning is not a good idea. I remember when Tom and I first made it to the west coast of the Penobscot Bay. I was so excited

---

[2] These early days of planning trips would be extremely helpful in later years when we took two months to move *Makai* from Charleston, South Carolina to Pepperrell Cove, Maine. Without these experiences, I would have struggled to organize such a long-distance trip.

that I wanted to sail across the bay to Vinalhaven Island immediately, but Tom made the point that we had a plan to return to our home port by a certain date, and if we took the chance of crossing the bay and ran into bad weather or other problems, then the situation could become stressful. Whether you need to be home for work, your daughter's ballet recital, or your mother's operation, stick to your plan as best you can.

Tom and I took off for Provincetown one bright, cool morning and got underway. As we sailed toward Cape Anne Tom reviewed some information about the buoyage system that we would depend on for safe sailing. Some of it I already knew. For example, on my first sailing trip I had learned about red nuns and green cans. The "red-right-returning" rule was that you pass red markers to starboard (on your right, facing the boat's bow) and green ones to port when traveling up a river or into a harbor. When leaving a river or a harbor, the sailor applies the system in reverse.

Red markers are conically shaped. They are referred to as *red nuns* and have even numbers on them. On a chart you might see something like, "R N 2" which means a red nun buoy with a "2" on it. Green markers are cylindrical in shape, have odd numbers on them, and are called *cans*. "G C 3" means a green can buoy with a "3" on it. Matching up what you see on a chart with what you see in the water provides a valuable way to reckon your location.

Photo 6:1 Red Nun
Red nuns are common sights while underway. Sailors match which
nun they see with nuns on their charts to ascertain if they are on course.
Nuns have even numbers, and green cans have odd numbers on them.

Cans and nuns were not the only markers we would see on our trip.
We entered lots of harbors, and many of them had offshore buoys in
front of them. These are usually taller than cans or nuns and are red and
white. "RW G" means the marker is red and white striped with the letter
"G" on it. We also saw lighted markers. If a marker is lighted, then it
will flash when it is dark or foggy. "G 1 Fl 4" sec means that the marker
is green, it has the number "1" on it, and it flashes each four seconds.

Other offshore buoys we came upon were gongs and whistles.
These might identify a specific location or a hazard. When we were
sailing in fog, there was nothing more eerie than coming on one of
these huge markers, whistling mournfully in the mist as we passed by.
And it was usually a welcome sight too because as we moved cautiously

through the fog, we were searching anxiously for any marker to verify our location.

On our way to the Annisquam River, we passed some New Hampshire sites that were familiar to us from the land. Wallis Sands Beach, Rye Harbor, and Hampton Beach went by before we approached the long, sandy stretch of Plum Island and entered Ipswich Bay and then the Annisquam River-Canal that divides Cape Ann from the Massachusetts mainland and connects the city of Gloucester to the Annisquam. When we got there, traffic picked up considerably, and we were surrounded by many small powerboats that rushed by us. I wanted to look at all the beautiful homes that lined the river, but found I had to concentrate on helping Tom with navigating.

At the Annisquam Yacht Club, about a half a mile south from the entrance to Ipswich Bay, we picked up a mooring for a night. We had some dinner and then watched a group of laughing young people jump in a bevy of the club's sailing dinghies for an evening race. They energetically wove in and out of the boats on their moorings. Up early the next morning, we found it was chilly, and I brought to the cockpit steaming mugs of coffee which we sipped as we made our way down the river. Before long we passed through a railroad bridge and then a second bridge, and soon found ourselves sailing southwest into the long, narrow harbor of Salem (see 70.896 west longitude 42.519 north latitude). When we arrived we thought about picking up a mooring in the outer harbor, but decided it would be too far for Tom to row to get to the town dock.[3] So Tom called a local marina on the radio and arranged for us to secure some dock space at Pickering Wharf.

I had never docked before, so Tom reviewed with me what we would do. (See Side Bar 4:1 on Docking and Mooring Your Boat.) I was to put a line on the port side of the bow and another on the stern's. Then I was to hang three fenders (an inflated cushion used to protect the side of the boat) from the safety lines on the port side so that they hung down to protect the hull of the boat from bumping against the dock. Tom would

---

[3] We did not yet have an inflatable dinghy with a motor on it.

be at the wheel, and I on the bow, as he nosed along side the dock. I would throw the bow line to the waiting dock hand, then hurry to the cock pit and throw the stern line to him or her. The dock hand would secure the lines on large cleats on the dock. This sounded easy enough. However, it did not exactly happen that way. Later I was to realize that very little goes the way you plan it when docking and, consequently, I always feel anxious whenever we plan to do this maneuver.

In the first place the wind was against us from the beginning because it was blowing across the dock, forcing Tom to exert engine power to bring the boat in. This caused the boat to crash against the dock in spite of the fenders I had put out. Second, there were no dock hands. I have learned over the years that it is wise to assume that Tom and I will dock the boat ourselves. If someone is around to help, fine. But it doesn't pay to expect that. In Salem, there was no one around so I gingerly leaped from the side of the boat to the dock with the bow line which I tried to quickly secure to a cleat. I was not fast enough, and the boat's stern, blown by the wind, swung away from the dock so that the boat was nearly perpendicular to it. Tom rapidly threw me the stern line. I lunged and caught it before it fell in the water and, bracing the line against a cleat, I tried to slowly pull *Northstar* toward the dock. It was hard work. I pulled the stern line a little, cleated it off, ran to the bow line, pulled that in a little, re-cleated it, ran back to the bow line, and pulled that in some more, and so on. Tom could do little more that shout encouraging words as I dragged the boat in, literally, inch by inch.

Once the boat was securely positioned to the dock, Tom ran spring lines which restrain the boat from surging forwards or backward. To do this he attached lines from the base of the mid-ship stanchion (the post that supports the safety lines) to the aft cleat on the dock. Then he attached a second line from the genoa winch in the cockpit to the forward cleat on the dock. Once again, see Side Bar 4:1 on docking for more details.

I was panting and exhausted by the time the boat was safely on the dock. And it did little for my humor or my dignity to look across the marina to see three or four people sitting on the back of powerboat watching us and laughing heartily. I was very cross for a couple of hours.

Salem is a great town, and we took a full day to explore it. Although sailing can in fact be just about sailing, on a passage it makes for a richer experience if you build in fun things to do on land. (See Side Bars 10:1 "Surviving Being Stuck on Shore," and 10:2 "Sailing and Life-Long Learning.") This can be especially rewarding if you are traveling with children. Learning about history, art, ecology, and so forth in this way makes it come alive to a young person in ways that it doesn't in the classroom, or even through books or films.

Salem lends itself especially to this kind of experiential learning because of its notorious past. Founded in 1626 by some settlers from England under the leadership of Roger Conant, it remains a colorful and dynamic port, filled with history and beautiful architecture and gardens. We visited the Custom House where Nathaniel Hawthorne, the great American writer, worked in the early nineteenth century. During his life, Salem was a port for the clipper ships which went all over the world. The Custom House played an important role in managing the goods brought in by these ships and in increasing the wealth and prestige of the area. We also passed by the House of the Seven Gables on Derby Street that Hawthorne made famous in his novel by the same name.

I fell in love with the Peabody Essex Museum. It was founded in 1799 as the Salem East India Society. Members collected materials from all over the world to display there. Later it became the Peabody Museum, and in 1992 it merged with the Essex Institute to become the Peabody Essex Museum. This is a world-class museum with both art and historical artifacts. It is an enchanting place, and once there, it was hard to tear myself away.

Of course Salem is known for the witch trials of 1692, and there are at least two places you can go to learn more about them. The Salem Witch Museum presents a powerful play about these tragic events, and the Witch Dungeon Museum shows the trial of the beggar woman,

Sarah Good. Guided tours of the dungeons where the so-called witches were kept are available. There is a relatively new memorial for those killed because of witchcraft allegations. It is simple and effective. These visits will be of special interest to children who might love the idea of witches and the supernatural.

Before Tom and I walked back to the boat, we stopped at an Indian restaurant and had a curry that was spiced with something I had never tasted before. To this day, I don't know what the herb or spice was, but it was exotic and delicious. For some reason, the visit to Hawthorne's Custom House, learning about the clipper ships which traveled to China, all the talk about seventeenth-century witches, the dinner and spices, and the general atmosphere of the port of Salem made me feel that we had fallen into a different time.

After dinner Tom and I strolled back to the boat through the harborside shops and boutiques that lined the water. We sat out for a little in the cockpit, but one of the disadvantages of being on the dock rather than being on a mooring or on anchor is docks tend to be full of people walking around. There are also bright lights that illuminate the area for security and safely. The people and the lights, along with the realization that the tomorrow was going to be a long day, compelled us to turn in early.

The next day we headed for Scituate which lies south of Boston. We sailed across Boston's wide bay, a long trip with the city in the distance. When we arrived in Scituate and found a mooring behind the breakwater, I felt a sense of relief. But then I made a terrible mistake. I let go of the mainsail's halyard – the rope that is used to pull the mainsail up to the top of the mast. Normally when the mainsail is lowered, we unclip it from the sail and secure it by wrapping it around a winch and tightly cleating it. But that day, I unfastened the end of the halyard and let go of it so that it ended up at the top of the mast, meaning that we would have no way to raise the mainsail, and thus no way to use the mainsail for the rest of the passage. I can't imagine what I was thinking. ASA 2010, p. 31 even includes a special warning about not doing this, which I had read.

When Tom realized what I had done, he tensely explained that we would not be able to raise the mainsail unless we got the other end of the halyard down from on top the mast. I was mortified. I watched miserably while Tom detached the topping lift (a line which secures the boom to the top of the mast) and attached a rope to it with some metal hooks. He raised the lift and the rope and caught the halyard with one of the hooks. He then pulled on the rope and dragged down the halyard with the topping lift, securing the former to the top of the sail and the latter to the end of the boom. Now everything was back in its proper place.

All of this took a certain amount of time though. And it was tedious work with me watching through binoculars and guiding Tom's efforts. Both of us were silent, trying to imagine the rest of the trip without the mainsail. You can imagine our relief when we got things back to normal.

This incident illustrates an important point about sailing. Problem solving and patience are key habits-of-mind to cultivate if you want to be an effective sailor. Whether your boat is the grips of a lobster pot or your mainsail halyard lies by mistake at the top of the mast, there are many ways to solve the problem. You just have to imagine them, see if they work, and if they don't, come up with a different solution. And sometimes this will take days. Of the two of us, Tom is the better problem solver. He is extremely inventive and does a good job of "thinking outside of the box." On the other hand, I read directions better, and sometimes that can be very important, such as when you are putting in a new hot water heater on the boat.

After recovering somewhat from our ordeal, we rowed the dinghy into Scituate and took a short stroll around the center of town before returning to the boat and preparing dinner. We were exhausted. We had another early night, and the next day we ("bravely" in my case since I would be out of sight of land on a sailboat for the first time) headed across Massachusetts Bay to Provincetown which lies on the northern tip of Cape Cod, southeast from Scituate. Tom had already made this trip once in *Trull II,* but it was all new to me. It was about 30 miles of open water, and I felt very intrepid.

SIDE BAR 6:2 WAYPOINTS,
GLOBAL POSITIONING SYSTEMS (GPS), AND CHARTPLOTTERS

Knowing how to use GPS technology and chartplotters can make you a better sailor. Think of waypoints as route junctions encountered when driving on a trip. Maps instruct you to take route I-495 to route I-290 etc. In the case of the ocean, lakes, rivers, or waterways, waypoints, markers placed by the federal or state governments, represent the junctions. For example, when leaving Pepperrell Cove, pass red flashing buoy "2" on your port side; it marks Whaleback Reef. Then pass Whaleback Lighthouse before heading for marker "2KR," which is a red flashing whistle buoy. It is also kept to port when traveling Down East. Each of these markers has its own unique location specified by longitude and latitude. All of these markers are found on charts. The only problem we ever had with this was in Casco Bay when the government reclassified some of the markers which made for some anxious boating.

When planning a passage, find the places you want to stop and locate markers near to them. Then find other markers you'll pass on the way to these stopping places. Many of the Chart Kits list the markers at the back of the book with their coordinates. But a waypoint need not be a marker. It can be an empty piece of ocean that is the optimum place to change course. You can create these waypoints using your ruler and compass on the chart. Use the latitude scale on the right and left and the longitude scale on the top and bottom of the chart.

GPS units are very helpful. You can enter these markers into the unit before leaving your mooring. Then simply follow one marker to the next, even in dense fog. I recommend that you find the actual markers to verify the accuracy of your unit. Don't "cut corners" or make assumptions.

If you choose not to use, or do not have a GPS unit, which can be costly, plot your trip on charts with course degrees for each leg. As you proceed, check your speed and calculate how long it will take to sight the marker. Remember, currents and wind alter the course, and while your compass tells you what direction you are traveling in, it does not give you your location. The GPS unit keeps track of where you are at all times and makes adjustments to your course as you proceed.

Chartplotters are another helpful aid to sailors, but they, like GPS, can be costly. They display an electronic chart on a colored screen and incorporate the data from the GPS readings onto the map. They allow you to zoom in and out so that you have at your fingertips a large amount of information to process. I recommend that when you input waypoints into your GPS and on to the chartplotter that you take some time to carefully zoom in to each section of your trip to familiarize yourself with it and to take note of any problem areas.

Tom knows how to use a sextant, and I do not. What follows is somewhat technical. You can skip over it unless you plan on committing yourself to learning this technology. If you do celestial navigation, you will need a sextant to shoot several sun sights and cross these lines of position with your DR (Dead Reckoning -your course traveled). Tom suggests that 9:00-9:30 sights (sun and possibly moon), noontime sights (Meridian Passage) and 3:-3:30 sights (sun and possibly moon) give you good information. The Meridian Passage sight works if you have a good time piece or have recently received time ticks from WWV, the national radio timepiece. Start 15 minutes before noon and follow the sun up and down until 15 minutes after noon. Interpolate the readings to get absolute "local" noon. This tells you your longitude within the local 15 degrees (1 hour of sun travel) of your time zone. You can also calculate your latitude using the Nautical Almanac by comparing your angle for the sun at noon to that for the specific day in the Almanac. Tom says that sun sights are good fun, and with a little practice you can do them quite quickly and plot the LOPs on your chart.

Sailing technology has changed dramatically over the last fifty years. However, it is unwise to rely just on "high-tech" features, forgetting the underlying principles of navigation. Having paper charts on board along with a set of parallel rulers and dividers remains a very good idea…just in case.

It was a hot, still day with little wind. We used the spinnaker, and it worked very well for several hours. We enjoyed watching it from the cockpit until we realized it was tugging us off course, so we took it down and relied on a combination of motor and sail for a while. Towards the end of the afternoon we spotted land, and Tom explained to me that the lay of land can be deceptive when you first come upon it from the sea. We would have to be careful because what we were seeing might not be what we thought it was, and we could damage the boat if we made wrong decisions. Tom <u>thought</u> we were seeing Race Point at the very end of Cape Cod, which meant we would sail south, passing it on our port side and then curve around, heading northwest past Long Point and into Provincetown Harbor. He was correct, and as we approach the harbor, we started the motor and took in the sails. It was after five when we picked up a mooring at a marina. However, without the GPS we rely on today and the certainty that it brings, we could easily have been mistaken. This made me think about sailing in the era between 1500 and 1900. Those sailor/explorers were brave indeed.

I had reached our destination on my first passage. I was quite thrilled and very proud of myself. After having a quick dinner, we called the marina's launch which motored us to the dock. It was dark, and we walked past lighted shops and boutiques. Provincetown's downtown is full of Cape Cod-style shingled houses and cottages, many of which have been turned into stores. The shops were full of everything from fudge to books and designer clothes to jewelry.

Art galleries were everywhere. Provincetown established an art community in 1914, and over the years it has evolved into a vibrant colony. Today there are not only galleries where local artists' works are sold, but the Provincetown Art Association and Museum (PAAM) allows you to view the full range of artists who work in the region.

The next morning we rented a couple of bikes and rode out to Race Point where we sunbathed before we visiting the National Seashore Park which had an informative visitor center. It explained how the area has been settled and deforested which allowed for serious erosion of the dunes and land. The park service was fighting to restore and maintain the dunes.

We biked back into town, stopping to have a late lobster lunch. It was late afternoon, and we noticed that a wind was increasing, and clouds were racing across the sky. We went back to the town dock where the launch picked us up. As we bounced through the frothy waves toward our boat, the launch driver warned us that a storm was imminent.[4]

Remember that I was a novice sailor in those days. I thought we must hurry back to the boat because there was a storm in the offing. A more seasoned sailor would have known the misery of being on a moored boat when a storm passes through. Such a sailor might think that it would be a better idea to check into the nearest hotel until the storm ended, assuming that the boat would be safe enough on a solid mooring. Maybe it was better I didn't realize all of this because I'm sure that Tom wouldn't have joined me in a hotel because he would have felt

---

[4] This trip took place before the Weather Channel existed or before there were accurate long-range predictions of what weather would be like. It may seem extraordinary to us today that we lived through such precarious times, but live through them we did. (And I'm certain it was only worse in the 1700s.)

disloyal to abandon the ship at such a time. That would have left me in an awkward position because I would have to choose between the boat where Tom was and the hotel where I would be comfortable.[5]

That night in Provincetown I did not have to face such a choice because I was pretty "green." Happy in my ignorance I jauntily stepped onto the boat and entered the cabin. Within a few hours the wind was howling, and the seas where making *Northstar* violently buck up and down. Rain slashed against the portholes and hatches. We could barely eat a thing since we were both sea-sick, and the power of the winds and water made it impossible for us to read or even listen to anything on the sound system. Tom said he was going to bed and climbed into the forward bunk. I tried to follow suit, but the bucking and jerking seemed worse up there than in the main cabin. So I remained on a bunk in main cabin wrapped in a blanket. I have to say it was a bloody unpleasant night during which I only slept fitfully. The hours crawled by.

Yet, the sea is an extraordinary thing. It can kick up furiously in hours, but afterwards, it calms down much faster than I would have thought possible. By the next morning, the wind and seas dropped, the sky was a fresh deep blue, and the sun shone. It was if the nightmarish night had never happened.

We went into town and visited a funny little aquarium and some shops before having dinner and returning to the boat. The next morning we got up early and started on our trip home. I now felt like a seasoned sailor.

As Tom and I crossed Massachusetts Bay on our way back to Scituate, friends of Tom radioed us from their powerboat. We told them our location, and within minutes we saw them streaking toward us. They pulled up along side of *Northstar*, and the two men got in deep discussion about weather and electronic equipment while the man's wife and I chatted about living on boats. They had been vacationing on Cape Cod, and Tom's friend, while out fishing, had remembered that Tom

---

[5] This experience foreshadows another that took place many years later.

would be sailing to Provincetown. He took a chance and radioed and was very pleased when Tom answered. He also proudly showed us the bluefish he had caught and offered us one. We accepted (could there be any fish that's fresher?), and he quickly cleaned it for us and handed it over. They waved as they sped off.

Tom and I continued on to Scituate where we had the bluefish for dinner. We then crossed Boston Bay and passed Salem where we had stopped before, and sailed on to Gloucester which lies on the south end of the Anisquam River-canal. Gloucester is a real working/fishing city where fishing boats and cruising vessels share the harbor. We anchored and went into town where we took a walk. Then we returned to the boat to eat and turn in.

At about five or six in the morning, Tom, who is a light sleeper when we are on anchor, heard something and jumped out of the bunk. He raced up into the cockpit and yelled for me to grab my clothes and come up. I hurried as fast as I could and climbed the stairs two at a time. I arrived just in time to see a large sailboat bearing down on us. Apparently it was on anchor, and the anchor was dragging. Tom and I did our best to fend it off so it would not damage *Northstar*. It slid by us, and we watched it go helplessly. Other boaters behind us had heard the commotion and were preparing to protect their boats as we had. This mystery boat seemed to have no captain. And yet leaving such a boat alone on anchor seemed to be the height of irresponsibility.

SIDE BAR 6:3 STARGAZING FOR INFORMATION AND FUN

When at sea or on anchor, you will find that the stars have never seemed so bright. The absence of ambient light and the freedom from trees and buildings provide breathtaking vistas of countless stars. After a while, you will find, as did our ancestors, that many of them seem to group into configurations which make it easier to find them again. This is where our signs of the zodiac come from: Pisces, Sagittarius, Scorpio, etc.

Stars can be useful when sailing long distances with one or more nights at sea. Finding a star that you can use as a beacon is preferable to constantly gazing at the compass, pretty though the lovely, rose nightlight is. But because most stars change their position as the earth rotates, they can't be used as reliable navigation tools.

The North Star, on the other hand, is unique. Its position does not change since the earth revolves around it. So, if you happen to be traveling from Boston to Bar Harbor, or, as Tom did, from St. Thomas to Bermuda, the North Star is a beacon to steer by.

It is easy to find the North Star by first locating the Big Dipper. It is a group of seven stars that looks like a saucepan and handle. Follow the two stars that make up the front (opposite the handle) of the saucepan, and there you will see the North Star. It is not the brightest of stars, but it is clearly visible on most nights. The value of the North Star is that it gives quick reference to north, if you need it.

In any summer in New England, interesting star clusters can be located using the Big Dipper. When you follow the handle, a very bright star, Arcturus, becomes visible. It also seems to blink with red and green lights. Tom told me a funny story about when he and his crew were sailing *Makai* from St. Thomas to Charleston, South Carolina. They were sure Arcturus was a helicopter. They only figured out what it really was when they noticed that it didn't move.

From Arcturus look for a ring of stars, the Corona Borealis (Northern Crown) and continue to a super-bright star Vega. This star is part of the Navigator's Triangle, which is generally overhead in summer in the Northeast. The three stars that make up this triangle are Vega, Altair and Deneb. Also in the New England cosmos in summer are the signs for Scorpio and Sagittarius. They line the southern horizon with Scorpio's curl sweeping along the night horizon. The bright star in its neck is Antares. It is the target of Sagittarius's arrow (to the left of Scorpio on the horizon).

All of these stars are candidates for celestial navigation. They can be brought down with your sextant to an artificial horizon and processed using the Nautical Almanac and Hydrographic Office publication (HO229 tables) to get a line of position to cross with your DR (Dead Reckoning).

Have fun, find your sign in the sky, and discover the many stories in mythology that are part of the beautiful world above you.

Soon we set sail for Portsmouth Harbor. It was going to be a very long day because we were traveling past a third of the coast of Massachusetts and the entire New Hampshire coast. There was little wind and no seas to speak of, and the trip was quiet and uneventful. When we reached my beloved Whaleback lighthouse, the sun had already set, and the lightest possible breeze pushed us gently by it. We sailed into Pepperrell Cove as the purple-shadowed twilight surrounded us. And when we picked up our mooring, neither of us wanted the moment to end.

Chapter Seven

The Magic of Casco Bay

Casco Bay has always been a magical place for me. The rocky islands and smell of pine mark it as something very different from southwestern Maine. Plus it has the attractions of Portland, a city with much to recommend it. Yet, it is frequently covered with fog, which can make sailing challenging, but because of the beauty of the region, most sailors agree it is worth the effort to explore it.

Our travels in Casco Bay taught me an important sailing lesson: that of flexibility. It is important for sailors to plan routes and anticipate whatever obstacles might be thrown in their paths. But even when you do your best planning, "things happen," and you might need to make changes. I have found that it makes absolutely no sense to press forward with some plan when the costs of doing so may jeopardize the safety of the crew and/or boat.

On our first trip to Casco, Tom and I were so excited that we got underway in the greyness of the early morning. As we dropped our mooring pickup pole in the water and motored out of Pepperell Cove, small, black-hooded laughing gulls flitted around the boats. Since efforts to control the black-back and herring gull populations have been successful, we are seeing more terns and laughing gulls in Pepperrell Cove. (See Side Bar 5:5 Gulls and Terns.) This has turned out to be a mixed blessing, in that although the laughing gulls are lovely to watch as they dive and turn over the waters, I find their raucous cries to be loud and unmusical. Plus, they sit on the booms of boats and make terrible messes on the dodgers, sails, and cockpits. We ended up having to create a tent-like structure of tarps over the back part of the boat to protect it when we weren't on board.

The morning Tom and I headed for Casco Bay, we sailed northeast into the ocean much farther than usual, and then set a course for Saco

Bay. We rapidly left our usual sailing grounds behind us, being too far off shore to distinguish Cape Neddick, Bald Head Cliff, and Cape Porpoise. By noon we approached Saco Bay where we planned to spend the night in Biddeford Pool (see 70.352 west longitude 43.453 north latitude) and then continue on to Casco the next day. Seeing the Wood Island Light, we turned to port sharply, passing between Wood and Gooseberry Islands where a rocky point with a stick and green triangle mark the passage between the two. After turning on the engine and taking down our mainsail, we carefully motored west into the harbor where moored boats lay bobbing in columns. We avoided the sand bar and mud flats on the starboard side, while widgeons raced around us. Their hulls and red-striped sails reminded me of Japanese paper lanterns as they flew through the water.

Weaving our way through the young people and their small boats, we motored through a narrow straight and pulled into the small, inner harbor, called the "Pool." Biddeford Pool is well protected from seas and winds from any direction. We motored by dinghy into the local yacht club to sign in and pay for the mooring. The yacht club is housed in a lovely, old, grey shake-covered building surrounded by fragrant rugosa roses. Window boxes with red geraniums dress up the building. Nearby is a well-stocked market and a trail that leads along the coast through an Audubon Society-protected area. Along the way we saw plenty of gulls and terns and discovered raspberry and blueberry shrubs laden with ripe fruit. We ate some of them, savoring their sweetness in the sun-drenched sea air. This was a "special sailing moment," one of those times when you don't think you could have possibly experienced that instant anywhere else or at any other time than that moment, in Biddeford Pool, on that walk.

The next day was overcast, and the color of the sky and water were a steely grey. The winds were from the southwest, and we hoisted the mainsail and pulled out the genoa on the starboard side. We did not sail for long, however, because fog set in as we passed Old Orchard Beach. So we approached Prouts Neck at the north end of Saco Bay and picked up a mooring to wait for the fog to lift.

SIDE BAR 7:1 FOG NAVIGATION

Taking on fog voluntarily is not a good idea. If it is foggy, stay put where you are, even if it means you have to call into work to let them know you'll be late showing up after a vacation. Least you take fog lightly, Sleight (2001, p. 255-7) refers to "the terrors of fog," which I think puts it in perspective. If you are out on the water in fog and are not sure if a fast-moving powerboat or a huge tanker is headed your way, then it can be very unpleasant. I know. I've been there.

The American Sailing Associaton (2012, p. 132) suggests that you should use your own commonsense in predicting fog because weather channels may not be able to foresee foggy conditions since they might be local. By commonsense, they mean that if it is hot and humid inland, and if the wind blows the hot air over the cool seas, then fog may well occur. This may seem simplistic, but it is a helpful rule to remember.

Sleight (2001) and Maloney (2003) give advice about what you should do immediately if fog descends upon you. They urge you to take note of the boat's position, presumably by reading the GPS coordinates. Then make sure your radar reflector is attached as high as possible on your mast. Ask crew members to put on their life preservers on and assign individuals as lookouts on the port, starboard, and bow of the boat. Maloney stresses that hearing is even more important than seeing in foggy conditions. Thus, he suggests you shut off your engine every couple of minutes to hear anything that may be approaching. If you are on a medium-sized boat, make sure your dinghy is nearby and put the dinghy motor and supplies in it in case a collision occurs. If you are in a small boat, then check that the life raft is ready for release and that it has flares in it. If you have radar, make sure it is on, but maintain your lookouts. Don't make the mistake of depending one hundred percent on "high-tech" equipment because they are only tools in the hands of human beings who must interpret and understand the information they provide, and then act wisely.

Sleight makes some interesting observations about how you should proceed depending on where you are when the fog overcomes you. He suggests that, if you are out to sea, continue on course slowly, making appropriate sounds every two minutes (we had a bell and an air horn that was very loud). If you are in a shipping lane, as we were once in busy Portsmouth Harbor, get into shallow water as quickly as possible where a large vessel would not go. Anchor there until the fog lifts, and watch for other small crafts that might have the same idea. When we got in the path of a tanker coming out of Portsmouth's port in the fog, it blasted us, and Tom, being experienced, steered our sailboat quickly over to the east side of the harbor (the opposite side from Fort Constitution and the lighthouse there) until the vessel passed.

Maloney (2003, p. 360) offers some helpful advice that I wish we had known when we were on cruise with two other parties and fog descended upon us up around Boothbay. It was "pea soup," and our three boats were cautiously motoring toward Boothbay Harbor. We were in the lead and in radio contact with the other boats.

> The people in the second boat were clearly nervous and called to us repeatedly about speeding up or slowing down, depending on how their boat was managing. Maloney suggests taking advantage of a procedure used by wartime convoys. Each boat in the group, except the last, should tie onto the end of a long line something buoyant, large, and colorful such as a yellow life ring or a large plastic bottle and tow it from the stern of the boat. A lookout on the bow of the boat that is following will see it before seeing the boat and be able to guide his or her helmsmen with hand and arm signals.

After an hour or so of sitting in the clammy fog, we went by dinghy into a small but friendly yacht club. From the people we talked to, we learned that Winslow Homer, the famed American nineteenth-century artist, had lived and worked on Prouts Neck along with his father and brother. We walked up a hill to his studio which looked out on the water with breathtaking views. There were no paintings in the studio, but there were posters of his work done in Maine as well as in the Caribbean. We lingered there, appreciating the freedom we had to explore his studio and to imagine what his life must have been like, perched there on the rocky coast.[6]

By the time we returned to the boat, the fog had lifted somewhat so we decided to go on. Before hoisting the sails and releasing the mooring line, we turned to our charts and the GPS. The GPS gave us our position in degrees of latitude and longitude, so we knew precisely where we were. Beyond Prouts Neck, there lie only Richmond Island Harbor and Seal Cove before Cape Elizabeth which marks the beginning of Casco Bay. At Cape Elizabeth, we planned to turn north and approach Portland Harbor. We debated whether or not to go into Portland Harbor and pick up a mooring at a yacht club we read about in our sailing books. But we decided to save Portland for the end of our cruise, so, instead, we continued traveling northeast to Harpswell Sound (70.004 west longitude 43.757 north latitude) in the center of Casco Bay.

---

[6] In 2012 we drove to Portland to have lunch with sailing friends, and could not resist visiting the Portland Art Museum, one of our favorite museums in the area. We discovered that the Museum had purchased Winslow Homer's studio, had it reconstructed, and were in the process of organizing small groups to travel to Prouts Neck to tour it. They also planned a major showing of the artist's works that fall.

Using the charts we determined a route by which we would get to a point south of Harpswell's entrance. Of particular concern was a nasty smattering of rocks, ledges, and smaller islands that lie to the southwest of the Merriconeag Sound, through which we had to pass. We noted the coordinates of one of these features – Halfway Rock- which lies midway between Cape Elizabeth in the southwest and Cape Small in the northeast. A 76- foot, granite lighthouse stands on it. As I study the charts from that time, I can see that we circled a string of whistles, nuns, and cans that led vessels safely around Cape Elizabeth and West Cod Ledge just east of the cape. After passing through these, the charts indicate that taking a 39 degree course northeast would take us safely past Halfway Rock and on to Harpswell Neck.

Tom and I were a bit uneasy about the notorious Halfway Rock, having read about its history in sailing books and online. It had the unpleasant reputation as a "killer-of-sailors" and "wrecker-of-ships" well into the nineteenth century. Even ships that were careful perished on Halfway Rock. One poor captain, coming in on a stormy night, reefed his sails, determined to wait for daylight before approaching Casco Bay because of Halfway Rock. However, his ship was pushed in by the seas and landed on the rock nonetheless. He was killed but some of his men survived on the island until morning came, when they were rescued. Another famous boat from Scotland was apparently clueless and fell on the rocks suddenly. All perished. It was not until the 1870s that the United States government agreed to have the lighthouse built of granite brought in from Maine's quarries. In 1871 it was lit for the first time. Until it was automated in the mid-1900s, three lighthouse keepers were assigned to it. They rotated their service, two there on the island and one on leave. But even today with the lighthouse and its modern conveniences, ominous comments such as, "The island is subject to fierce storms" strike fear in the hearts of novice sailors like me (www. uscg.mil/history/weblighthouses/lhme.asp).

So Tom and I set off from Prouts Neck in the intermittent fog. We were confident that we knew our location and where we wanted to go, but where was everyone else? In fog this question become critical. That's where radar comes in. Theoretically, on the radar screen you should be able to see anything that you approach or that approaches you. It provides a bearing and the distance between a boat and any object around it. If the object is another vessel, then you can determine not only its relation to you, but also how fast and in which direction it is moving.

**SIDE BAR 7:2 RADAR
(RADIO DETECTION AND RANGING)**

When I first started sailing with Tom many years ago, he showed me the passive radar reflector on the mast of *Trull II*. He explained to me that it increased the visibility of his sailboat to other ships' radar. If he had not had this on his mast, then other ships and boats with radar may not have detected his boat in the fog or the dark.

By the time Tom and I acquired *Makai*, he began to seriously think about buying a radar system, especially since we were making passages further Down East where fog is a significant factor. Radar gives you the ability to "see" things that are on the water and/or on the chart and to ascertain their distance from you. It helps you avoid collisions and establish your position on a chart. It does this by sending out radio waves which pulse out and then are collected as returning echoes and displayed by a receiver on a screen mounted near the helm. For example, reflections from buoys, ships, the shore line, and other obstacles register on the screen.

However, as I have noted elsewhere, using radar is not as easy as it seems in the movies. It is an acquired skill that takes practice. It's a good idea to practice using it when you don't need it. For example, use it on a sunny day when fog and dark don't threaten your safety. Get used to the monitor, to how things look in reality compared to how they look on the screen, and to how moving objects, such as boats, show up on the monitor and pass you. If you still don't feel comfortable with using the technology after practicing, taking a course might be beneficial.

Radar systems for sailboats like *Makai* consist of two units: one with an antenna, transmitter, and a portion of the receiver which are placed in a unit as high on the vessel as possible, and one with the rest of the receiver and the monitor which are placed near the helm where it can be easily seen. Tom placed a pole on the stern of *Makai* and attached the antenna unit to it. This means that the mast and the shrouds are part of the immediate radar field and clutter the center of the radar display screen. However, since we are looking for objects beyond the bow of the boat, this has not proved to be a serious problem. He put the receiver/monitor in the companion way, under the dodger and protected from the rain. When we are not under sail, it folds back against the bulkhead and is covered with a waterproof cover.

I am somewhat ambivalent about investing in radar systems. If you intend to do significant overnight cruising, to dabble in blue-water sailing, or are on a schedule which requires you to be certain places at certain times no-matter-what, then purchasing a radar system makes sense. But if you are a small-sailboat owner who likes to do day sailing or racing in the harbor or a medium-sized boat owner (like we are) who cruises but has no rigid schedule, then I'm not sure I would strongly urge you to spend the money on a radar system. Having said that, Tom reminds me that our radar system has worked for us on many occasions and provided us with good information about boats and other obstacles around us, thus contributing to our greater safety and security.

Radar provides a way-of-knowing about the environment that is different from other methods, and I found it harder to use than I expected. Its depiction of things can be difficult to understand. I discovered it was not like in the movies when the captain of some vessel looks at a screen and sees a yellow dot moving toward his ship. The radar screen I looked at required a trained eye. And once you figure out what you were seeing, it can be hard to locate the feature on the water. For example we were looking for a whistle off of Cape Elizabeth, just south of Pine Tree Ledge. We could see it on the radar, but we just could not find it. Tom watched from the port side, and I from the starboard. I strained my eyes, my entire body tense with watching. Neither of us saw it until we were right on top of it. On the other hand, I hoped that power boats and large ships had and understood radar. I envision the captain of the boat seeing us appear on his or her screen and taking action to avoid a collision. (At least that was my hope, but maybe they had even more trouble reading their radar screens than I did?)

After leaving Prouts Neck and circumventing Richmond Island Harbor and Cape Elizabeth, we headed northeast into the heart of Casco Bay. The fog grew thicker, and *Makai* crept along with just the mainsail up. In the fog there was no wind to bother about, so we used the mainsail to stabilize the boat. On our 39-degree northeast course, after passing West Cod Ledge, we avoided Halfway Rock (that is, we never saw it in the fog but neither did we crash into it) and, with some relief, we motored more confidently into Merriconeag Sound toward Harpswell Harbor.

Harpswell Harbor is a broad open bay that is protected and has good ground for anchoring. We took the mainsail down and motored into the harbor where we tucked the boat into Stover Cove across from Orrs-Bailey Islands. The combination of the fog, the quiet seas, and the protection of the cove made it hard to believe we were actually on the water. And since we were the only ones in there, as evening set in, the tranquility was complete.

When a boat is on anchor, captains are loath to leave their vessel for any amount of time or to go any distance. If an anchor drags or the wind kicks up, the boat could be in danger. However, that night in Stover Cove, the fog, still air, and absence of seas allowed Tom to feel comfortable enough to suggest that we use the dinghy to cross the Sound to Orr's-Bailey Islands to search for a restaurant for dinner. I had a flash light and a horn so that if we saw another boat coming at us, we could signal it. Once we were near Orr's Island we saw a yacht club. We left our dinghy there and started walking. In time we found a seafood restaurant, and before long we were seated in front of a warm fire, enjoying being out of the fog with a Maine crab dinner and a white Bordeaux wine. That night we slept deeply and well. The strain of the day along with the quietness of the cove allowed us to relax and rest.

The next day the fog lifted, and we sailed from Harpswell to the New Meadows River. Sebasco Harbor is located about four miles north of Cape Small which is the farthest point east in Casco Bay. There is room to anchor there, or moorings are offered at a nearby resort. We dropped an anchor and motored in by dinghy to walk around the area. The air was cool, and the fresh smell from the pines gave it a vivid "Maine" feeling.

Tom and I headed into the New Meadows River the next morning and made our way north along the coast to what is called "the Basin." This is a wonderfully secluded and enclosed harbor with tree-lined shores about three miles north of Sebasco. We entered this amazing place through a narrow channel which opens up into what looks like a protected pond. After dropping an anchor, we sat back in the cockpit to enjoy the tranquility around us. There were no other boats and no visible houses on the shore line. We felt like we were the only people in the world with just birds for company.

Toward the late afternoon we took the dinghy and motored along the shore exploring. Along the way we saw seals swimming determinedly across the Basin. If we got too close to them, they went under the water. Otherwise they ignored us. Huge white-headed ospreys circled around us far up in the sky. A large nest buried in the upper reaches of the tree tops was clearly visible. The two parents took turns fishing and then taking the food back to the shrilly-peeping offspring.

By sunset the mosquitoes were out, and we retreated into the boat where we made dinner. There are many jokes about how large Maine grows its mosquitoes, and some sailors claim that the rule of thumb is, for every degree north latitude you travel, add a half an inch to the size of the mosquito. I believe that saying to be true after spending the night in the Basin.

All sailors establish their own night routines when on board. Melville in <u>Moby Dick</u> included wonderful descriptions of drinking rum and making merry on the forecastle (fo'c'sle)[7] of the whaling ship on which he worked. Tom and I tend to read, listen to music if there is a station we can find, or listen to audio books. Listening to audio books, especially murder mysteries, is our favorite because we can talk about

---

[7] The crew members of merchant vessels were housed in the fo'c'sle (the forecastle in the bow of the boat). This tends to be the most uncomfortable part of the boat when there is bad weather because the bow bobs up and down in the waves (as I discovered in Provincetown, Massachusetts during a storm). The captain and his staff's quarters were located in the stern of the boat, which is relatively stable compared to the bow. I noticed in my readings of the maritime literature that many captains such as Ahab strung up hammocks in their quarters to sleep in. Charles Darwin, while on his five-year stint on *Beagle*, also slept in a canvas hammock – once he figured out how to get into it. While sleeping in them, the rough seas were hardly noticeable because the hammocks tended to counteract the motion of the boat.

what we are listening to and speculate about motives, characters, and villains. There in the Basin that night, we listened to a story, and when we thought the mosquitoes had disappeared, we crept out on board to gaze in awe at the star-studded sky that surrounded us.

The next morning Tom and I regretfully began to make our way back west. We passed Harpswell and cut north through Broad Sound, leaving Chebeague Island to our port side and stern. Lower and Upper Goose Islands and the Goslings lay ahead of us. This unique grouping of islands has much to recommend it. If you tuck the boat behind the shelter provided by the two smaller islands (the Goslings), pointing south, you'll find the bottom is mud and provides excellent holding ground. Lower Goose Island is the larger of the two, but Upper Goose Island is owned by Maine's Nature Conservancy and protects the largest great blue heron colony in New England. Hundreds of nests have been spotted in the trees on the island. Unfortunately during the summer months, the interior of the island is off limits because of the breeding cycle of the birds. However you can walk on the gravel beaches of the island, or just use your dinghy to explore its coast. To get a glimpse of a group of these giant birds, soaring majestically over the water with their legs held in back of them is a quite an experience.

The next day we proceeded on toward Harraseeket River and the town of Freeport. We passed between Stockbridge and Moore Points, keeping the delightfully-named "Pound of Tea Island" on the starboard side. When I was at the wheel, I steered my way along our route, keeping the green cans to port side and fervently thanking heaven that I had taken my lessons on buoyage systems seriously. It seemed to me that the smaller the area you boat in, the greater the number of markers. For example, the channel into Freeport was only about a nautical mile long, but there were five green cans and three red markers – two nuns and a flashing light at the entrance to the channel. I was nervous that I would bump the bottom of the boat on a rock or something. In the muddy-bottomed Waterway of New Jersey or in the Chesapeake, that would not be catastrophic, but rocky Maine is a different story altogether.

In Freeport, we picked up a mooring and went into the dock where an outdoor restaurant was crowded with people. We waited on line and took a couple of lobsters to a picnic table where we spread out in the sun and fresh air. The lobsters were delicious, and the butter we dipped the morsels in was hot and fresh. After our meal we had to decide whether or not to take a shuttle or a cab into the factory outlet area that L.L. Bean has made so famous. In the end we opted not to because of the crush of people. Instead we walked around the town before heading back to *Makai*.

The next day we continued west on our way to Falmouth. The views in the protected waters of Casco Bay were spectacular. Homes, boats, and scenic natural vistas dotted the shores. Chandler Cove, between Long and Chebeague Islands, leads to Clapboard Island. To the west, toward the Maine coast, lies the large Handy Boat Marina, but we did not pick up a mooring there. Rather, we contacted the Portland Yacht Club, the country's second-oldest yacht club. They had an empty mooring available for us, so we motored there, and Tom grabbed the pickup pole. After settling in, we went to the dock and walked around but found no real town center, only streets of houses. The yacht club was somewhat more elaborate than what we were used to, and we had dinner, sitting outside at tables where we could view the water.

The city of Portland lies just to the south. We could have sailed straight down into Portland Harbor, but it was such a lovely day that we decided to sail between Great Diamond and Peaks Islands in the Diamond Pass. The air was fresh and clear, and the views of the houses, trees, and rocks were beautiful. Then *Makai* headed for Portland. The tempo definitely picked up as we neared this large and dynamic port. Ferries charged back and forth, and commercial vessels dwarfed sailboats like ours. We entered Portland Harbor, steering clear of the traffic, and saw the city stretched out before us on the hills.

As we hoped, the yacht club in South Portland we had read about had a mooring for us. The club is on the south side of the harbor, and Portland is on the north side, so we had a marvelous view of the entire city. We spent the rest of the afternoon puttering on board. I washed out some clothes and hung them to dry; Tom tinkered on the engine. We called the club launch to pick us up so we could take showers in the club house. The facilities at the club were simple, but we appreciated them. Then we returned to the boat to read and listened to music as the sun set.

Next to the yacht club a marina with a nice restaurant tempted us with an interesting menu. We walked to it and were given a comfortable table with a view of the marina and harbor. That night on the boat, with all of the lights of the city before us, we sat in the cockpit and talked about the passage. We both had enjoyed Casco Bay and thought we would return in future years. It was late before we turned in, hating for the evening to end.

The next day was one of our layover days, and Tom and I asked the yacht club's launch driver to take us across the harbor to a large marina's dock that we could see from our boat. Carrying our two-way radio with us to call for him to pick us up later, we proceeded to walk around the downtown area. There were a lot of shops on Front Street as well as interesting antique stores. Art galleries sold oil paintings and watercolor pieces of Maine. I was tempted to buy one, but Tom reminded me that we would have to carry the painting to the launch, motor it to *Makai*, and then use the dinghy to transport the painting to the car when we got to Pepperrell Cove. Besides, where would we stash it once we were on board? I gave up on the idea.

We found a jazz music shop on one of the streets that stretched perpendicular to the harbor docks. We spent a good hour there going through old cassette tapes and CDs. The two men who owned the shop were agreeable and did not mind chatting with us about their favorite artists.

This shop became one of our regular haunts, and every time we stopped in Portland at the end of a cruise, we walked up the hill to visit the shop owners, and purchase a few CDs. Just recently, however, we went to the store and found that it had gone out of business. We were sad to see it go.

Another place we discovered on that trip was a real gem. The Portland Art Museum is located at a convenient walking distance from the docks. It is not a "monster museum" that takes weeks to go through like the Museum of Fine Art in Boston or the Metropolitan Museum of Art in New York. Rather, it is a modest size that always has a special exhibit which we make a point of visiting. One exhibit we saw was entitled "Monet to Matisse, Homer to Hartley: American Masters and Their European Muses." It was a perfect exhibit for our cruise because the two American artists, Winslow Homer and Marsden Hartley (1877-1943), had been so inspired by Maine's scenery. And, of course, we had just visited Homer's studio on Prouts Neck and seen copies of his works of the ragged coast line and the turbulent seas. Hartley's paintings, more abstract in their expression, communicated the essential power of the forests and the bodies of water that so distinguish Maine.

Another exhibit we visited marked the centennial of Rockwell Kent's (1882-1971) arrival on Monhegan Island. The exhibit was excellent with over 150 different works that had been assembled from places as far away as the Hermitage Museum in Russia. The paintings were not only of Maine, but of Greenland, Alaska, and Tierra del Fuego where he rendered images of glaciers, mountains, and the ocean. We lingered over this very special exhibit which seemed to resonate with our experiences in Maine.

In Portland, you can walk everywhere. After a few hours in the museum, Tom and I walked back to the docks, stopping at a casual restaurant, which had a great raw bar. Tom had some oysters on the half shell, and I had a cup of clam chowder that tasted like it really was home-made. The dominant spice in it was thyme. It was unusual, and I enjoyed it.

Down on the docks, we used the two-way radio to call the launch driver who came across the harbor and picked us up. He dropped us off at *Makai*, and after a late dinner we sat out again watching the city lights.

The next morning we motored out of the harbor and around south Portland toward Cape Elizebath before hoisting the sails. We headed southwest towards Stage Harbor. The wind was unfortunately on our nose, so we had to beat for the next 25 miles. But the seas were not too bad. They were huge lazy swells, and *Makai* sedately made her way down the coast with little trouble.

We arrived at Stage Harbor in time to walk on the beach. Tom brought a little pail, and we searched for mussels on the rocks and under the seaweed. We quickly found about a dozen, and after a refreshing swim in the chilly water, we went back to the boat and steamed them over a beer-chicken bouillon broth that we were first introduced to in a restaurant in Portsmouth. They were very tasty and made a great first course before dinner.

The distance between Stage Harbor and Pepperrell Cove is 25 miles, and the next day we made it home in about five hours or so. The maximum speed we attained on that leg of the journey was six and six tenths nautical miles per hour. We motored some of the way because the wind was still out of the southwest. But we managed to get in some good sailing too.

All-too-soon, we were back on our mooring, commending ourselves on a great passage. Casco Bay had turned out to be filled with surprises. The contrast between the serenity of the Basin and the bustle of Portland was extraordinary. The rocky islands and sweeping bays were a change from the sandy coast of southwest Maine which we knew so well. We had defied the fearsome Halfway Rock and survived. We had met up with fog and managed to cope with it either by depending on equipment or by waiting it out. It had not spoiled our cruise. We had practiced using radar, and I had more experience charting our courses for the day. I had done some excellent work on applying what I had learned about buoyage systems, and I was feeling increasingly confident about trimming sails. Although I could not yet call myself a "real" sailor, I now had a better idea about what a "real" sailor was, something I hadn't understood before. So all-in-all, I was definitely making progress.

Chapter Eight

Maine's River Region Between Casco and Penobscot Bays

For several sailing seasons Tom and I were happy with Casco Bay and even now we plug in a trip to Portland on the way home from a passage or stay a night in tranquil Harpswell harbor before proceeding home to Pepperrell Cove. But the time came when we began to look beyond Cape Small. The next natural destination for us to think about were the rivers that lay between Penobscot and Casco Bays. They are the Kennebec, Sheepscot, and Damariscotta Rivers. Plus Boothbay and Linekin Bay lie just east of the Sheepscot River, and John's Bay with Pemaquid Harbor and Muscongus Bay are situated east of the Damariscotta River. St. George River is located at the most easterly point before entering Penobscot Bay. Exploring this vast, rich area took years of summer sailing, and we still do not know everything we'd like to know about the region.

As Tom and I traveled on the rivers, we continued to have to contend with fog on a regular basis, but the new "add on" that we had to learn about concerned the powerful currents that rule the lives of boaters who venture on these waters. We already had some experience with currents because the Piscataqua River is known for its strong ebbs and flows. This thirteen-mile long river drains quickly, and tidal currents average three knots on the flood and five on the ebb. For example, if we are at Dover Point up the river on our way down to Kittery and Pepperrell Cove, then we have to determine not only when the tide will be at its lowest so we can pass under Memorial Bridge without smashing our mast, but we must also plan to travel with the ebbing tide. Otherwise the force of our motor will not be able to overcome the force of the water as it floods into the river headwaters. The same principle holds for motoring upstream. Go with the river as it floods upstream, and not against its waters as they ebb out toward the sea.

Each river has its own personality, and it was important for us to recognize this and treat them with respect. We were warned about the Kennebec River's currents, and the Damariscotta River, at full strength, has currents that flow up to five knots. There is also a constriction of the Damariscotta about four miles from the mouth, and the currents are particularly powerful there. The St. George River is much easier to navigate, but upstream near the town of Thomaston, the river narrows considerably. Knowing this, and planning accordingly, helped us considerably.

So our exploration of the rivers began. Tom and I rounded Cape Small and sailed south of Fuller Rock which is marked by a 25-foot high flashing light. In the distance we saw Sequin Island and the lighthouse which guards the mouth of the Kennebec River, marking the dangerous Sequin and Jackknife Ledges (see 69.768 west longitude 43.745 north latitude). This lighthouse is the oldest island lighthouse in Maine and was constructed in 1797 and reconstructed in 1857.

The Kennebec's mouth is intimidating, and I always approach it with some trepidation. Giant slabs of rock stretch out into the water from the craggy shores on both sides, and strong tidal currents create a nasty chop that tosses *Makai* around as if it were a feather. Although the scenery is magnificent, it is also formidable.

The first time we approached the Kennebec River was quite a shock. All of a sudden the current, the result of a strong ebb tide, seized *Makai* and turned it around. We quickly started the motor and got the boat under control. Then we rolled in the genoa and pulled in the main sheet so that the mainsail was in the center of the boat. With the boat thrashing around the way it was, it was impossible for Tom to go forward to secure the mainsail. We inched our way through the mouth of the river. *Makai* became sluggish, and we turned the throttle up as high as we could. I crossed my fingers hoping that we would not be thrown against the towering, rock slabs and founder.

Don Johnson (1986, p. 79-80) provides text that gives you a sense of what the average sailor is up against at the mouth of the Kennebec. He describes the current velocity of the Kennebec River as two to three knots, sometimes reaching six knots on the ebb tide. However, the velocity isn't the only problem. The strength of the current continues for a significant distance from the mouth of the river, and when it meets winds coming from the opposite direction, then an extremely heavy chop builds up, creating white water. This is not only dangerous to small boats; it can threaten larger vessels too. Add to this the large shoal area that extends south and southeast from Pond Island. Johnson advises sailors not to attempt to enter into this area in any kind of heavy weather or fog. Rather, go outside of Sequin Island as you head Down East or on your return. After citing every warning he can, Johnson adds, almost as an afterthought, that if the weather is clear, then the inside passage between the Kennebec River and Sequin can be quite beautiful.

Well, I have to say, going through the passage between the mouth of the river and Sequin was always quite an experience, and we motored or sailed through it any number of times. And, oddly enough, I came to look forward to being terrified at that part of a passage and was disappointed if we sailed around the outside of Sequin. I can't explain it, and it seems counterintuitive, but there you have it.

Once we got beyond the mouth, we discovered that the Kennebec was just another friendly river. Also once away from the sea breezes, we found it was quite warm. We found a tiny inlet, anchored the boat, and went swimming. The spot was perfect, and the water was so fresh that we spent an hour at least enjoying ourselves.

About 12 nautical miles from the mouth sits the town of Bath. The Bath Iron Works continues to construct new ships there, and the Maine Maritime Museum, where we picked up a mooring, is involved with conserving the history of boating and its unique culture. We arrived in

Bath in the late afternoon, and I was tired from swimming and from doing battle with the mouth of the Kennebec. The maritime museum was closed because it was so late, but a jamboree of vintage cars was taking place on the museum grounds.

The museum itself is worth a visit. Nineteenth century coastal Maine has a rich history, and the exhibits imaginatively describe it. Nearby are the Iron Works, which is identifiable because of the huge cranes and its industrial atmosphere. Bath's downtown is small, but there are shops and restaurants. I remember particularly that there was a big kitchen shop there. We went in and bought a small wooden cutting board for *Makai's* galley.

The next morning we timed the current carefully knowing that it would take hours to make the 12 knots to the river's mouth if we went against the tide. As the river emptied we dropped the mooring ball and felt the current take the boat. We had the engine on, but we were going fast even with it in neutral.

As we approached the mouth of the river we saw with dismay that the heat had caused a blanket of fog to form. It enveloped the town of Popham and its adjacent beaches, and it was beginning to drift up the river. I really did not feel like braving Sequin Island, the rocks at the mouth of the Kennebec, and the possibility of a dangerous chop --- all in the fog. It was the last straw for me. Tom agreed, so we motored over to Popham's town dock. A fisherman was pulling in at the same time, and he kindly pointed out a mooring he knew was empty. We grabbed it hoping that it would be heavy enough to hold the weight of *Makai*. At least there were no strong winds even if the current was powerful.

The next day, as we waited for the fog to lift, we went in and walked on the beach. We brought our bird book and identified terns, plovers, and a number of different kinds of gulls. Our book said we could expect to see gannets, kittiwakes, ducks and loons out at sea, but the fog prevented that kind of visibility. We also found a fort that had been built in the nineteenth century and walked around it before returning to the dock and having lobster.

By the following day, a cool breeze blew away the fog, and we left our mooring ball behind. Once clear of the giant rocks, we turned east and went into the Sheepscot River whose mouth is as wide as a lake (see 69.691 west longitude 43.868 north latitude). The wind was up, and there were white caps on the waves. Luckily there did not seem to be such a problem with currents in the Sheepscot, probably because it is such a wide river.

Tom and I had not put up a lot of sail, so once up the river we motored west into Goose Rock Passage which is a narrow corridor with a strong current that leads into Riggs Cove and the much-larger Robinhood Cove (see 69.736 west longitude 43.834 north latitude). A small sailboat, perhaps 20-feet long, was struggling in front of us. As we passed him with our stronger engine, we waved. He grimaced back at us, and I wondered how he would fare in the mouth of the Kennebec River.

Photo 8:1 Robinhood Cove
Picturesque Robinhood Cove provides a comfortable place from
which to explore the area. At night the stars are unusually bright.

On the shore of the Riggs Cove lies a marina with a restaurant. We took the dinghy into the marina through clear green water to talk to the dock hand. We had hot showers, bought ice for the ice box, visited the library where we exchanged some paperbacks we had read, and then walked over to the restaurant for dinner. After dinner we walked along a tree-lined road up to the small cape that juts into the cove, almost dividing it in half. A "no trespassing" sign stopped us however, and we regretfully turned back. On our way Tom spotted some chanterelle mushrooms which he gathered and used to make an omelet the next day.

Another time we stopped at Riggs Cove we borrowed a courtesy car and drove around. We found a restaurant in an historic white building. We didn't have reservations but they were able to seat us at a small table next to a window that looked out onto a garden with orange daylilies. The sun had not yet set, and the curtains fluttered in the warm breeze. It was beautiful. I ordered duck, and Tom had lamb. It was "fine dining" at its best, and all the more enjoyable because the restaurant and its surroundings were so unexpected.

That evening we sat out admiring the broad sweep of the cove and the forested shores that hid any of the homes that might be there. We saw at least two large blue herons and a green heron fishing intently near the rocky shore line. As twilight deepening, a raccoon came down to the water and fastidiously pawed under the exposed sea-weed-covered rocks for tidbits to eat. At one point it found a large curtain of kelp that shrouded what seemed to be a small cave. It entered into it and came out about ten minutes later. We wondered what it found in there.

Once the light from the setting sun faded complete, it was pitch black. There were no lights from houses, nor was there a moon. But then we saw a fabulous panorama of bright stars spread out across the sky. We were able to distinguish the entire constellation of Scorpio which we can only see in the summer. Riggs Cove seemed to me to be one of the more idyllic places we visited while sailing in Maine. Years later, it continues to be one of my most favorite spots.

The next day we motored about ten miles up the Sheepscot River to the lovely town of Wiscasset which used to be a shipbuilding and lumber port but is now a scenic town with lots of antique shops and a charming art gallery. It was settled in the early 1700s and was a major shipbuilding center. The many grand homes built by wealthy sea captains attest to it being a thriving port at one time. Wiscasset has a different personality altogether than does Bath which retains its working-class energy. It is a gracious place with streets of historic houses laid out around the water. Many of them had wonderful gardens that were filled with late-summer-blooming flowers such as daylilies and monkshood.

I remember that Tom was at the wheel when we reached the town, and I went forward to grab the pickup pole of one of the public moorings. The current was quite strong, and I had to move fast to get the line through the hawsehole in the hull and secured on its cleat. We ended up staying in Wiscasset for several nights because we listened to the marine weather and heard that the weather had turned bad, with gale-force winds and high seas. So we settled in to enjoy ourselves on our layover days.

The next day it was stormy and unstable with lots of thundershowers and humidity. I have a photo of Tom and me in shorts with our bright-yellow, foul-weather jackets thrown over our shoulders walking to the Maine Art Gallery. Afterwards we ducked into a restaurant and had sandwiches and Maine blueberry pie as we waited for the shower to blow by. That afternoon we took the Maine Coast Railroad on a scenic tour of "Maine's mid-coast." The trip took two hours, passing through tidal rivers and marshes where we saw osprey, heron, and eagle nesting grounds.

The next day found us in Ebenecook Harbor which is south of Wiscasset across the river from the Goose Rocks Passage (see 69.682 west longitude 43.836 north latitude). There is a marina there that has changed hands several times, and the village of Southport is nearby. We checked in at the marina and walked up the road past an old graveyard, the historic society, and a bakery. A general store sold pizza, deli goods, and basic supplies. An unusual river beach with distinctive rock formations lay nearby. On our way back, we saw signs for the Hendrick's Head Trail. The path took us into a forest where we saw pink and pale green moss on the ground and silver-green lichen on the trees. As we returned to the boat Tom searched for more chanterelle mushrooms. His success at Riggs Cove had wetted his appetite. But we found none.

Ebenecook provides access to Townsend Gut which is a shortcut between Sheepscot River and Boothbay Harbor. It is a narrow slot with a bridge. The trip is scenic, easy, and short. We liked the views and had no trouble with the swing bridge. There is a rock right after you go through the bridge on the east side of the channel. You have to watch for it and keep the red nun to port as you go along. Most recently the bridge was undergoing routine maintenance and painting which happens every twenty years. So on that trip we had to go around, down through the mouth of the Sheepscot and up into Boothbay Harbor.

While exploring the Sheepscot River we spotted a black guillemot which is a pigeon-sized black bird with white wing patches and red feet. We had not seen this bird in southwestern Maine, so we were excited. Another bird we saw on this trip was the Wilson's storm petrel which breeds in the southern hemisphere and visits the northern hemisphere in the summer. This is an ocean bird, and once away from land, it is quite plentiful. It's about seven inches long and skims the sea showing its distinctive white rump. (See Side Bar 1:3 Birds).

Boothbay Harbor is large tourist-friendly town that is usually crowded in the summer months. A myriad of shops and restaurants keep you busy. One time we spent a couple of lay-over days there, staying in a marina on the dock. Most recently we picked up a marina's mooring ball on the east side of the inner harbor. We went in for showers and then walked over to a nearby restaurant. We were given a nice table on the verandah and watched the well-known windjammer cruise boat come in packed with people enjoying themselves.

The following day, we continued east. Directly east of Boothbay Harbor is Linekin Bay. We don't usually stop there but we have heard that it offers quiet sailing and peaceful anchorages. We pressed on to the Damariscotta River which is the next major river you reach after traveling past Boothbay and Linekin Bay.

Near the mouth of the Damariscotta is lovely Christmas Cove. This immensely popular and well protected haven is approached by passing through a constricted point carefully marked for boaters. Ospreys have made a nest on the green marker, and a juvenile indignantly peeped at us as we came too close to him. Inside the cove lie moorings that are managed by a marina with a restaurant. We called ahead on the radio and discovered that they had an opening, so we motored up the river and got ourselves settled. We were grateful because there were a lot of boats, and no room for anchoring inside the cove.

There are some lovely walks around the cove. We strolled up to the main street and turned onto a quiet lane. A short walk brought us to a small market which sold berries, deli supplies and canned goods. We walked back to the marina and explored another lane which led to a point where beautiful homes with marvelous views lay. In one garden we saw an elderly man tying his gorgeous purple-blue delphiniums to stakes. We stopped and commented that we had never seen such beautiful flowers which, I think, pleased him.

It looked like it was going to rain, so we hurried back to the restaurant where there was also a casual bar. We went in to have a glass of wine before dinner. I saw a huge dog laid out in the hall way with a tiny five-year-old boy fondly petting him. Every time it thundered, the dog whined with fear, and the boy comforted him.

Dinner was nice, and the rain had stopped by the time we finished so we went for a short walk before going back to the boat. The air was clear and smelled like fresh pine. When we arrived back to the boat, the people in the neighboring vessel informed us that our boat had nearly collided with theirs during the shower. They apparently had had a few anxious moments fending off *Makai* while we were serenely eating in the restaurant. We apologized saying that the mooring balls seemed to be placed too close together. Later I made a note that when we returned in future years we should not accept either of those mooring balls because of the lack of adequate swing room.

The next morning we took another walk before taking off for the village of Damariscotta. We crossed the island of Rutherford to visit the town of South Bristol, which is a working town. Boats of lobstermen and fishermen crowd into what they call The Gut. This is a narrow thoroughfare connecting the Damariscotta River with St. John's Bay, and a swing bridge allows traffic to drive between the island and town.

The rest of the day was spent winding our way along the 14 nautical miles of river that separates Damariscotta from the ocean. It was spectacularly beautiful scenery. There were green scented forests and outcroppings of rock from time to time. I already mentioned previously that I saw seals sunning on some rocks during this trip. One of them was white; I had never seen a white seal before and was amazed.

The town of Damariscotta lies on the east side of the river, and the town of Newcastle is on the west side. A bridge connects them. The former is the hub of shopping for nearby villages and homes, so there are grocery stores, ATMs and pharmacies. There was plenty of opportunity for us to stock up on provisions.

We had a piece of luck in that a group was performing a revue of old Broadway songs in the town hall. We quickly purchased tickets and spent the afternoon listening to a remarkably professional performance. It was really great. Our only complaint, for ourselves and for the performers, was that it was atrociously hot. Fans were strategically placed around the room but they did little to dissipate the sultry heat. After the show was over, and we had shaken the hands of some of the performers, Tom and I walked out into the evening where there was the beginning of a pleasant breeze.

Later that week we took the dinghy and went up the river to Glidden Point where there are huge shell middens that were created by Native American over 2,000 years ago. It was high tide when we left, and we went under the bridge that divided Newcastle from Damariscotta. The middens were impressive; it was clear even from our amateur inspection that the occupation of that area was extensive and lengthy. We clambered around them before returning to the boat at the end of the afternoon.

That night we went out to eat and took a walk afterwards. Tom walked ahead of me toward the Newcastle-Damariscotta Bridge, and I heard him start to laugh. I caught up with him and asked him what was wrong. He pointed to the river. It was transformed. The placid stream we had enjoyed that afternoon was changed at low tide into a torrential cascade of rocks and white water. The roar of the water was tremendous. If we had returned to find those conditions, we could only hope the outboard motor would have gotten us to the shore of the river before we went onto the rocks. There is no way our inflatable dinghy would have survived that trip.

Soon it was time for us to make our way down the river and out into the ocean. We went around Rutherford Island and cut north toward the mouth of the Pemaquid River. At Pemaquid Harbor Fort William Henry has been reconstructed for history buffs. The area was settled back in the late 1600s by British. They had a rough time in the beginning because the Native Americans attacked them, but the settlers persevered. We have visited Pemaquid Harbor on several occasions. Its historical dimensions are interesting; there is a grocery store in walking distance; and it is protected from seas and wind. However, we have never lingered there.

East of Pemaquid Harbor lies Muscongus Bay. In stark contrast to Casco Bay, its islands look like little round buttons with tufts of green on them. I find them delightfully funny looking. If the seas are reasonable, we sail across the bay to Port Clyde where we secure a mooring from the general store. If the seas are difficult we cut into the bay and thread our way between the many islands. We have sailed or motored into Muscongus a couple of times, and it is challenging. There are so many small islands, and a million red and green markers stand ready to confuse even the most conscientious navigator.

Photo 8:2 Muscongus Bay View
Muscongus Bay is a complex area that offers
challenging navigation but beautiful views.

Port Clyde is an artistic town. If you like photography or painting, it will draw you like a magnet. It is small and hilly, and has great views and lots of art galleries. Our first day we walked to a hotel which was a three-story, clapboard building with a veranda on the first and second floors. On a patio in back, a restaurant served blueberry pancakes. We fell into conversation with a couple next to us. He was a watercolor artist, and she was his manager. They had wonderful stories to tell us about exhibits they had worked on. His goal in Port Clyde was to do some sketching and test out some new ideas.

The weather was so nice that after breakfast we decided to go back to the boat and take off on a river trip. Northeast of Port Clyde is the mouth of the St. George River. Thomaston is about ten nautical miles upstream. This town was founded in 1605 by an English man who recognized its potential for ship-building. By the nineteenths century it had launched more wooden ships than anywhere else in the country. Rich sea captains and boat builders built their homes and raised their families there. Today you can walk the streets lined with many of these grand old homes and visit the Maine Watercraft Museum to get a sense of bygone days.

Tom and I did not stay long in Thomaston but made our way back down the river to Broad Cove which is just northeast of Maple Juice Cove. We dropped an anchor off of Bradford Point and then took the dinghy to a wooden ladder where we tied off the inflatable and climbed up to a path that led us through a lobster pound to a road. Along the lane we saw houses with art studios.

Tom and I were discussing how scenic the area was and how fitting it was to see all of this evidence of creative art when we unexpectedly came upon an historical building. We went inside and discovered that the house was called the Olson House and used to belong to the family of Andrew Wyeth's (1917-2009) model Christina Olsen. It was there that in 1948 he painted "Christina's World," the iconic picture of Christina sitting in a field with her house and barn in the background. The house is open to the public, and the society that cares for it had done a good job of providing reproductive art works by Wyeth in places where he had actually done a painting. You can see what inspired him.

Outside Tom and I walked over to the small graveyard where Christina and her family are buried. For some reason I had imagined Christina as an isolated, ill person who did not have many means. But we found that she and her family were quite social and not poor at all. It is true that her ability to walk was limited, but that had not held her back from having a full life.

I walked back to the boat feeling richer than I had when we climbed the ladder at the boatyard. In that moment I saw clearly that the gift of sailing and exploration were intertwined and linked inexorably with beauty and creative power. It is true that you need technical know-how to sail successfully. You have to understand the wind and the sails. It is vital to be able to use navigational instruments such as GPS and radar. All of this is true and important to know. Yet, perhaps it is even more important to remember that sailing takes you to places in ways that you would not have experienced otherwise. You see things differently when you are sailing. In fact, you are different when you are sailing.

By this time in our sailing history, Tom and I were sailing past southern Maine altogether and, perhaps, visiting Portland in Casco Bay on our way home after our cruise. We focused our time on the rivers, coves, and bays in mid-coastal Maine. In our logs, I found one passage itinerary that looked something like this:

Day one:	Depart Pepperrell Cove; arrive Biddeford
Day two:	Depart Biddeford; arrive Ebenecook on the Sheepscot River (This was about 40 miles and took between 7 and 8 hours, depending on the weather.)
Day three:	Depart Ebenecook; arrive Seal Cove on the Damariscotta River
Day four:	Depart Seal Cove; arrive town of Damariscotta
Day five:	Layover day in Damariscotta
Day six:	Depart Damariscotta; arrive Maple Juice Cove on the St. George's River
Day seven:	Depart Maple Juice Cove; arrive Otis Cove on the St. George's River
Day eight:	Depart Otis Cove; arrive Ebenecook
Day nine:	Depart Ebenecook; arrive Snow Island in Quahog Bay in Casco Bay
Day ten:	Depart Snow Island; arrive Portland
Day eleven:	Layover day in Portland
Day twelve:	Depart Portland; arrive Biddeford
Day thirteen:	Depart Biddeford; arrive Pepperrell Cove

Just as an endnote to this chapter, in the log I cite above I read the following from day nine of our passage.

"We went out into the Sheepscot River to immediately confront four to five foot swells. We spent the next two hours sailing at a crawl toward Fuller Rock [off of Cape Small – marking the beginning of Casco Bay as you sail west]. Very grey, very heavy swells -- some as large as eight feet. I kept the helm to avoid seasickness. When we approached the Kennebec River and Sequin – as usual- the river current mixed with the sea swells to create a horrific combination. Surreal! We turned north after finally reaching Fuller Rock and sailed into calmer seas toward Quahog Bay. Deep inside the Bay we found Snow Island and tucked *Makai* behind it. Peace at last. What a hell of a battle. I'm exhausted."

Chapter Nine

The Vastness of Penobscot Bay

Tom and I had yearned to go to Penobscot Bay for years before we actually traveled there. That's because we were working with the limitations of a ten-day or so vacation from work. It takes several days of sailing to get Penobscot, and then to get back. That would leave only three or four days to explore the entire bay and no time for bad-weather layovers. So we held off until the two of us were able to break away from work for two to three weeks. Then we set off for Penobscot.

We sail-motored intensely the first couple of days, trying to cover as much ground as we could. The first day the winds were from the southwest so they were behind us. It was hot and humid, and big swells propelled us along. That night we anchored outside of Biddeford Pool, as we had done so many times before. The second day the winds were still from the southwest, and the seas built to four to six feet which made it hard to steer to the east. It was cooler though. That night we went up into Sheepscot River and stayed at Robinhood Cove. The third day we crossed the Sheepscot River and motored through the Townsen Gut which took us into Boothbay Harbor (see 69.635 west longitude 43.843 north latitude). We sailed out of the harbor and headed east. The swells continuing to build.

Makai zipped across Linekin Bay, the mouth of the Damariscotta River, and Muscongus Bay (pan between 69.613 longitude 43.805 north latitude and 69.261 west longitude 43.924 latitude). The swells were on the beam which made for rough sailing. I was slightly sea sick, but the speed and scenery were exhilarating. We made it to Port Clyde in four and a half hours with a maximum speed of 9.7 nautical miles per hour. Not to put too fine a point on it, we flew that day.

By that time we had been to Port Clyde a couple of times but in my log notes I wrote that I did not remember it being so beautiful. I compared it to a Marston Hartley painting where the ragged line of the evergreen trees juts into the sky with strips of grey-gold rocks lying beneath them. There is a wonderful lighthouse there too. The Marshall Point lighthouse was built in 1832, and today many artists who reside in this part of Maine are inspired by it.

Tom and I have sailed to Port Clyde in a number of ways. Because Muscongus Bay is complex, it is important to study the charts, enter the proper waypoints, and look sharp (see 69.379 west longitude 43.929 north latitude). Now is not the time to relax and listen to music. Once we set a course from Pemaquid Point in the west, straight across the Muscongus Bay to Eastern Egg Rock, then to Thompson Island, and past Hupper Island (leaving it to port) to Port Clyde. Going through the Egg Rock area is challenging because there are rocks and depths of 4 feet, 6 feet, etc. And the passage between Thompson and Davis Islands is narrow with shoals.

Another longer but less stressful course is to go south of the Egg Rock and Thompson-Davis-Allen Islands area. Once past, head north to Hupper Island and into Port Clyde. Of course if you are interested in a scenic tour of Muscongus Bay (which is well worth the trouble because the islands, bays, ledges, and coves are so beautiful), you can head north past Western Egg Rock, as we once did. Then, head north to Friendship Long Island, passing through Friendship Harbor and south past Gay Island and over to Port Clyde, leaving Hupper Island on your starboard side. Note that, although lovely, this requires concentration. We were tired when we got to Port Clyde from not only changing sail configurations constantly, but from watching for our markers. One island or cove looked very much like the next one to us, and since Muscongus Bay is so complicated, you must be sure about what you are doing.

The next morning Mussel Ridge Channel, which provides a relatively sheltered way into the Penobscot Bay, beckoned. We motored south from Marshall Point, then turned east, keeping Mosquito Island on the starboard side. We set our sails and turned off the motor, rounding the point and heading north towards the channel. As we passed Tenant's Harbor, Tom tried to turn the engine on for some reason I now forget. It did not respond. All we could hear was a clicking sound. We quickly decided to turn into Tenant's Harbor and drop an anchor or pick up a mooring so we could determine what was wrong (see 69.205 west longitude 43.963 north latitude).

As luck would have it, there were a billion lobster pots and a group of widgeons racing in the harbor. I was at the wheel, as Tom continued to try the engine, and did my best to weave my way between the pots and the boats, and although I tried to stay out of the way of the racers, I could tell from the expressions on their faces that some of the people were annoyed at us. At one point Tom called out to a couple who cut in front of us that we had no engine power. I couldn't tell if they heard him or not. We eased deeper into the harbor, and Tom pulled in the genoa and let down the mainsail. Then, as the boat slowed to a halt, he dropped the anchor. I thanked heaven that inside the harbor the seas and wind were modest. We did not have much to contend with, and our arrival was quietly graceful.

I must also mention a quality that my husband possesses that I envy. As we made our way through the harbor, I felt increasingly anxious. Would we run over a widgeon and kill two teenagers? Would we crash into a moored boat and do considerable damage? Would we not be able to drop the sail and control the speed of the boat to the extent that we could anchor successfully? Then what? Would we plow into the docks? Would we kill a family of four? Every single thing that could go wrong popped into my head. I turned to Tom and said frantically that I thought we should turn the boat around and get out of Tenant's Harbor. He considered the idea calmly for a moment and then said, no, he didn't think that was necessary. He then went forward nonchalantly to drop and secure the mainsail. And so we anchored. Well, the things you learn about yourself and your sailing partner while sailing would probably fill many volumes. I am definitely plagued by more anxiety than Tom is.

We spent a couple of days in Tenant's Harbor. Tom worked on the engine and came to the conclusion that there was something wrong with the starter switch. He eventually hot wired the starter so he could bypass the switch for the duration of the cruise. I, in the meantime, sat in the cockpit, read, and people-watched. At the end of each afternoon we went into town, walked around, and found a place for dinner.

Tenant's Harbor, as all the towns we have visited, has its own personality. It is not hilly and artistic like Port Clyde; and yet, the artist Jamie Wyeth (1946-), son of Andrew Wyeth and grandson of N. C. Wyeth, uses a lighthouse off of Tenant's Harbor as a studio. This lighthouse was purchased in 1978 by Andrew Wyeth and his wife who eventually handed it down to Jamie. The lighthouse figures as subject matter into paintings done by the two men.

Tenant's Harbor is also different from Rockland which is more of a serious working port. Instead, it has a relaxed genteel feel to it. While out walking we stopped at a lovely inn on the water that had a big veranda overlooking the harbor and garden. It had a wonderfully-spacious dining room with white wainscoting and sea-green textured wall paper. Our first night there we went in and were seated by a window that let on to a beautiful summer garden.

As Tom continued to work on the engine, I read some more in the cockpit and occasionally yelled down questions and encouragement to him. The views were scenic, and the air was balmy and warm. I was not unduly worried about the engine problem because Tom is mechanically inclined. By the end of the second afternoon he had solved the problem, telling me all about starters and solenoids (and other things I didn't understand). Since he was happily putting everything back together in the main cabin which looked like a cyclone had hit it, I didn't complain.

SIDE BAR 9:1 HOT-WIRING THE STARTER ON YOUR ENGINE

I need to preface this side bar by saying what follows is somewhat technical. If you don't understand it, don't worry. I'm not sure I could replicate what Tom describes, even with his careful instructions. However, we include this to give an idea about how you can approach engine problems.

Marine engines, diesels in particular, are very dependable machines. However, there are times when something goes wrong, such as when we first entered Penobscot Bay and had engine trouble. Tenant's Harbor was nearby, so as I mentioned in the text, we sailed into the harbor and anchored. Once we were anchored, the harbormaster came along side and told us we couldn't anchor there. We told him about our problem, and he let us use a town mooring for free.

In a case where the engine doesn't start or even produces the noise of trying to start, it's a good bet that the problem is electrical rather than mechanical. Tom

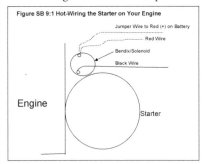

Figure SB 9:1 Hot-Wiring the Starter on Your Engine

believed that no electricity was getting to the bendix (solenoid) on the starter. He explained to me that the bendix serves two purposes. It provides power to the starter and lodges a bridge gear between the starter motor gear and the flywheel of the engine. Once the engine starts, the bridge gear retracts so that the engine and motor don't work against each other.

Figure SB 9:1 Hot-Wiring the Starter on Your Engine

This is a case for your multi-meter in the tool chest. Tom told me that he proceeded to, "set the meter at 20 V DC and place the red (+) lead of the meter on the red (+) pole of the bendix and the black (-) lead to ground (any clean metal engine part). I then had Debra turn the ignition key. The meter should have read 12-13 volts (battery voltage). When there was no reading, I knew that the ignition switch was not providing electricity to the bendix. The ignition wire carries low amperage. It is designed to close the shunt of the solenoid which carries the heavy current. I then attached a long piece of wire to the red pole of the bendix and had Debra set the throttle in starting position and held the other end of the wire to the red terminal of the battery. Voila!! The engine started, and we were able to continue on our way, jumping the engine when we needed it. I replaced the ignition switch when we got back at Pepperrell Cove."

Tip: To determine the red (+) terminal of the bendix, set the multi meter on 200 K ohms. This is the resistance gauge and reads 1 when the leads are not touching anything or each other. They read 0 when they are touched together. Once you are certain that there is no current going to either of the bendix contacts, place one lead on a contact and the other on ground (black battery terminal or metal engine part) If you get a reading of 0 then this is the negative contact and the other one is the positive one. If you get a reading other than 0 you are reading the resistance of the bendix and are testing the positive contact.

Our last evening in Tenant's Harbor, we took a walk and then stopped at a rustic place that served lobster and chowders. We were given a choice of eating inside or outside on the dock and chose the latter. As we sat at a picnic table facing the harbor with the boats bobbing in the dusk, they brought us trays of lobster with coleslaw, potato chips, and a large rock each. Puzzled we looked at each other. What was the rock for? I caught the eye of one of the helpers, and she came over and explained that they did not serve picks and crackers to break open the claws of the lobsters. You had to pound them open with the rock.

The next day, as promised, Tom jump-started the engine, I took the wheel, and we headed out of Tenant's slot-like harbor. It certainly was a lot easier going out under power than it had been coming in under sail. The pots were still unbelievably thick but I managed to thread my way through them. We proceeded north, sailing further into Penobscot Bay. We passed Rockland and Rockport, deciding to stop at one of these ports on the way back. This was the furthest east we had ever been. As I looked around me I decided that the scenery was more like Muscongus Bay and less like Casco Bay. It was certainly very different than southwestern Maine. It was rocky with hemlock and pine trees lining the shore, and the islands resembled buttons like they did in Muscongus. There was a serenity about it too.

Photo 9:1 Typical Maine Lighthouse Scene
Lighthouses on the coast of Maine can be frequently seen.

In the afternoon we pulled into Camden Harbor and secured a mooring (69.052 west longitude 44.208 north latitude). The harbor is wide, in contrast to Tenant's Harbor, and it was somewhat turbulent that day. We arranged for a mooring and radioed for a launch that came and picked us up. Camden has the reputation of being a hub of photography, publishing, art, and sailing, and it did not disappoint. We walked around town which was larger than we had expected with a lovely park, various shops, galleries, and, of course, grocery stores and pharmacies where we restocked our supplies. Back on the boat we watched a huge boat with a French flag and with what looked like its own uniformed staff pull in. Once it was attached to a mooring the people on board hurried down under. Through the night it was quiet and dark on board. The boat was gone the next day when we woke up. We wondered if it were on its way to Canada.

Tom and I woke to fog. We had a slow morning, and at about midday, the sun burned through the fog, causing it to recede somewhat. A long ocean voyage with the fog would not have been advisable, but we only wanted to cross the west part of Penobscot Bay to Islesboro Island. So we dropped the mooring line and took off. Once out in the bay the fog settled back in, but we had our radar and GPS which Tom quickly got working. We were only out in the bay for an hour or so, and soon we approached the southern end of Islesboro, with Seven Hundred Acre Island and Warren Island off of the port side of the bow. We easily slipped into Gilkey's protected harbor and traveled north, passing Ames Cove (see 69.073 west longitude 44.259 north latitude). Just beyond it, also on Islesboro's east coast, lay a small cove marked for anchoring on our chart. I tucked *Makai* up into the cove, just beyond tiny Thrumcap Island, and Tom dropped the anchor. Through the wisps of mist I could see large mansions on the shore. "Natives" refer to these houses as "starter mansions" because many who stay on the island for the summer have their "real" McMansions somewhere else. They view their summer places as "cottages." After Tom and I were convinced that the anchor was well placed, we took the dinghy to the island and found a place we could leave it securely. We climbed up to a road and walked along it until we reached a small village. A shop there sold ice cream. Munching on cones, we continued to walk along the peaceful road. It was great. There were no cars. It was quiet and still, and the air felt very clean and fresh. Occasionally we would pass other walkers who nodded and called hello. Otherwise a peaceful summer silence reigned. I have heard that life on an island has a special quality to it. I sensed some of it that afternoon.

The next day we left Gilkey Harbor and headed north to the charming town of Belfast (see 68.996 west longitude 44.426 north longitude). There was a good breeze so Tom hoisted the mainsail and let out the genoa on the starboard side of the boat. We had a nice couple of hours' sail, following the bay to the northeast. Once we approached Belfast Bay, we came about and sailed across it toward the town. We kept Steele Ledge to starboard. A twenty-foot flashing red marker warns boaters of the ledge which lies close to the north coast of the bay. We entered the Passagasawakeag River and contended with its strong currents, which are similar to Maine's other rivers we have explored. Because of the strong river currents as well as our plan to spend a few days exploring Belfast, we opted to call the harbor master on the radio to see if she had a mooring for us. She did, and arrangements were made quickly.

The next day was chore day. I don't do a great deal of housework while I'm on board. But I do attempt to keep the cockpit and main cabin swept, the towels and the bed linens clean, any mildew that might appear destroyed, and so on. At around noon we were ship-shape on board and decided to go into town and explore. Tom and I discovered that we could take a scenic railroad trip. So we walked to the railroad station and took a two-hour train ride to the imaginary town of Waldo. The engineer and his helpers described the history of the area and the importance of the railroad. Apparently Belfast is the seat of Waldo County, and in the late nineteenth century it was one of the main shipbuilding sites in the northeast, constructing about 300 ships that traveled the world promoting trade between the United States and other continents. The engineer also explained that in the past they staged a mock hold-up on the train, but they abandoned the act because it scared the young children. Indeed on our trip there were many families, and it was evident that the children were really enjoying themselves.

Later we walked over to the Belfast Museum which is more like an historic society. Two or three crowded rooms provide information about the Belfast culture. Like the engineer on the train, the exhibits informed us of what an important boat-building center Belfast had been between 1840 and 1860. While at the museum a small tour boat came into port, and a group of tourists gathered in front of it. We later saw advertisements for this tour which involved staying on board for several nights and traveling from port to port in the Penobscot Bay.

We took a walking tour of Belfast's historic district that we found to be very interesting (Johnson 1987, 57). I don't know a great deal about architecture, so I was fascinated to discover that the guide identified a number of nineteenth-century architectural styles. The wealth from shipping and trade was considerable, and the ship builders and captains built homes in the styles of "Greek Revival," "Colonial Revival," "Italianate," and "High Victorian Gothic." It turned out to be a lot of fun to go from house to house, trying to figure out the main features of each of these styles. Johnson also provides information about the specific architects for those who are better informed than I about architecture.

One thing I can say with certainty is that, when sailing, the pace of life slows down. You find yourself relishing mini-train trips, musty historic societies, and bird watching on a beach in the fog. Just the fact that you are walking rather than driving gives you the opportunity to see things differently in small coastal towns and communities that you would not have even bothered to visit otherwise since they are so far off the beaten track. There is a luxurious feeling about this that contrasts with the fast-paced American lifestyle which has become the norm in so many parts of the US.

Tom and I spent a couple of days in Belfast and then took off on a breezy, clear morning with no sign of humidity or fog. We got under way and hoisted only the mainsail since we were not going very far. We were headed for Bucksport which is about six miles from the mouth of the Penobscot River in the northeast corner of the bay (see 68.802 west longitude 44.573 north latitude). After motoring down the Passagasawakeag River, we passed Searsport on the port side, and turned north into the Penobscot River. As we approached the town the river veers west. Bucksport is on the east side, and imposing Fort Knox is on the west side of the river. Tom took us to the dock to fill *Makai's* water tank and to get diesel fuel. However, a large white powerboat followed us in and beat us to the dock. We picked up a mooring as instructed by the harbor master and waited our turn.

Bucksport is a real working town. To the west of the city is a large paper mill that is visible from the water. I immediately noticed that the downtown area was more built up than any of the other towns we had visited so far. There was a chain grocery store, a pharmacy, restaurants, a movie theatre, and a post office all in walking distance of the town dock. After doing some shopping we went to the movies. The theatre was a funny old building that was informally organized to show films. It reminded me of Damariscotta when we went to the revue of the Broadway hits.

While in Bucksport, we also went by dinghy to Fort Knox. The harbor master encouraged us to use the granite stairs on the other side of the river. He said we could tie off the dinghy on a metal ring and then climb the stairs and be inside the fort. This seemed promising so we motored across the river. However, unfortunately the harbor master had not mentioned that we go during high tide when the water would cover the deep mud that lay at the bottom of the staircase. We bravely took matters in hand, however. We shed our shoes and clambered out of the dinghy into the mud, dragging the dinghy to the stairs. Once it was tied off we climbed the stairs and searched for a restroom where we could wash our feet and put our shoes back on.

Photo 9:2 Fort Knox's Muddy Stairs
Tom climbing the muddy stairs of Fort Knox,
across the river from Bucksport.

After making ourselves presentable Tom and I toured the mammoth granite fort which had been built in the 1830s to protect the Maine shipbuilding industry from British invasions. The British seized control of the Penobscot River in both the Revolutionary War and the War of 1812, claiming the surrounding area for the British crown. Fort Knox and a number of other forts in Maine were built to prevent this from happening a third time, but Fort Knox holds the distinction of being the largest fort ever built in New England, having the capacity to hold 137 guns (Johnson 1987, 60).

Fort Knox has two levels. Most impressive are the mounts for the cannons. In addition to casements and powder magazines, there was a large interior parade ground where a group of men who were participating in a weekend reenactment of "life at the fort" had just arrived with their gear. Making our way around them, we toured the common soldiers' quarters, the officers' quarters, and the kitchen. The place was very well maintained and was used regionally for educational purposes.

Photo 9:3 Fort Knox with Bucksport in the background
Fort Knox was built in the nineteenth century to prevent
the British from taking over that part of Maine.

Tom and I had more luck getting back into the dinghy than we had getting out of it. We returned to the boat without dirtying our feet and had lunch in the cockpit. Then we dropped the mooring line and took off for Castine which lies south of the mouth of the Penobscot River on the mouth of the Bagaduce River (see 68.796 west longitude 44.386 north latitude). We motored down the river in bright sunlight, and, when we reached Penobscot Bay, Tom hoisted the main sail and pulled out the genoa on the port side. A frisky breeze on the beam allowed us to have a nice sail in the tranquil waters of the northern part of the bay before we turned into Castine. We grabbed a mooring at one of the boatyards and then went into town to explore.

Castine is on the National Register of Historic Places. Street after street of beautiful old houses from the Federal and Georgian periods grace the town. We walked up and down several of the quiet lanes but our favorite one was Perkins Road that wound along the water. Lovely cottages with gardens lined the narrow lane, and we were able to peek inside some of the windows.

During the time of our visit the downtown of Castine had a bookstore-café, a small grocery store, a museum where we stopped for an hour, and some other small shops. After we walked around we went to one of the inns which was named after the first trading post established in Castine by the French in 1613. We had dinner there, taking our time as a thunder shower blew past. Later we walked through the rainy streets to dump the water out the dinghy and make our way back to *Makai*.

The next morning we started out bright and early for Seal Bay which lies south of the Fox Islands Thoroughfare that separates North Haven and Vinalhaven, both having year-round populations that swell during the summer months (68.804 west longitude 44.089 north latitude). It was warm and sunny when we took off but during the afternoon it turned cold and overcast. We donned our jackets before we pulled into the bay and dropped an anchor. The harbor is beautiful with lots of grey-gold rocks and fir trees. There are few houses visible, and we saw no other boats while we were there. It was peaceful and remote without feeling lonely.

The next day we motor-sailed through the Fox Islands Thoroughfare to the other side of the Penobscot Bay. I thought there would be more houses and crowds than I saw. Our Maine guide book noted that Islanders differentiate between tourists (who arrive on the ferry and stay for the day) and summer residents (who stay the entire summer; some of them have houses that have been in their families for generations).

We came out of the west end of the thoroughfare and put out the genoa on the starboard side of the boat. The wind had picked up and was coming across the port side of the boat. Tom and I took our time and had a few hours of sailing before we set our sights on Rockport, a small town that lies between Rockland and Camden (69.073 west longitude 44.184 north latitude). It is another slot-like harbor like Tenant's, and we picked up what turned out to be a mooring far out in the harbor. When we used the dinghy to go to town for provisions and to drop off trash, it took us forever to get to the dock. After picking up some supplies we walked around the hilly village noting there was only one small restaurant within walking distance of the docks. It was closed, serving only breakfast and lunch. We dropped by Rockport's famous opera house and took photographs.

Back on *Makai*, we made a pasta dinner and sat out listening to music while the lights of the houses on shore around us blinked out. It was warm enough for me to take a quick refreshing swim off the back of the boat before we turned in.

After visiting Rockport it was time for us to think of returning home to southern Maine. We tried to stop at different points on our way back than we had on our way to Penobscot. We spent our first night at Boothsbay Harbor, our second in Portland, and our third in Stage Harbor. Before we knew it, we were looking for the Whaleback Lighthouse and preparing ourselves to arrive at our home port.

SIDE BAR 9:2 SEA BIRDS

Sea birds are different from the birds I see most of time around the house. Cormorants are large, dark seabirds known for their diving and fishing abilities. We frequently see them in Pepperrell Cove and while we are out sailing. They are easily recognizable because of their backwards-"S"-shaped necks, and the way they spread out their wings to dry in the sun when they perch on rocks. They also fly low over the water in a distinctive fashion.

The black guillemot, pigeon-sized, black with white wing patches, and red footed, is a bird we began to see as we traveled further east along the Maine shore. Apparently it is a hardy bird, living in the Arctic, where it is threatened by the retreat of pack ice (Peterson 2008, map 277). However, it breeds as far south as Maine during the summer months.

A charming bird that was new to us and that we first saw when far from our home port is the Wilson's storm petrel. At least, we believe we identified this bird correctly. It breeds in the Southern Hemisphere, and during the summer it visits the Northern Hemisphere. It is supposedly one of the most abundant birds in the world, nesting on islands in the ocean. We first noticed it because of the way it hovers over the water. It is only about seven inches long, black with a white rump patch and an un-forked tail. Apparently there is Leach's storm petrel too which has a forked tail (Bull and Farrand 1977, p. 321-322).

Regretfully Tom and I have yet to see a puffin. These spectacular birds are rare and threatened with extinction. They have big colorful beaks that resemble those of a parrot's, and they have distinctive eyes that look like snowflakes. They nest and reproduce in the summer in the coastal waters, usually on islands, and spend the winters out in the seas. Their home is the north Atlantic in places such as Iceland, Norway, and off the coast of north England and Scotland. Now there are nests closer to the United States, in places like Eastern Egg Rock off of Muscongus Bay and Machias Seal Island, southwest of Grand Manon off of Machias. Tours in nearby towns offer to take you there to see and photograph them.

As Tom and I took in the sails and motored over to our mooring in Pepperrell Cove, I thought to myself that we finally made it to Penobscot Bay after years of wanting to go there. Was I disappointed? No, I was not. The combination of fir trees and rocky ledges, quiet coves and small towns, rivers and the immense bay itself, offers a rich experience to boaters. As Casco Bay has become more populated, (some say, more exciting and vibrant; others complain that it is too crowded), Penobscot's dual personality of tranquility and rough hardiness stands unchallenged. It contrasts sharply with many other places where we have recently sailed.

Had I learned anything new about sailing? I certainly had been given plenty of opportunities to practice the lessons I had already learned. Traveling in the fog, figuring out currents, using the GPS to the extent that it felt intuitive, trimming the sails so that they took optimal advantage of the wind/current opportunities, and anchoring or picking up mooring lines were skills I practiced again and again. In Tenant's Harbor, I had confronted a crisis when the motor didn't start. Tom and I worked together to get the boat where it needed to be so it could be repaired. It is true that Tom was the one that figured out that the starter didn't work, but at least, once again, I discovered that problems happen, and problems can be solved. It is not the end of the world when the engine doesn't work (or something else goes wrong).

I will never be the sailor that Tom is. He has an uncanny instinct for the seas and for boat performance, and the years he has spent sailing off the coast and in the blue waters of the Atlantic Ocean and Caribbean have served him well. However, I was learning and, perhaps more importantly, enjoying myself as the sailing lessons unfolded before me.

Chapter Ten

"Down-and-Out" In Moose Island, Off Stonington, Maine

During the last week of July Tom and I started our passage for Bar Harbor, our next big goal after Penobscot Bay. We did not make it, but got held up on Moose Island close to Stonington (see 68.678 west longitude 44.150 north latitude). We had developed a rhythm whereby we usually took off sometime in late July, returning to our home port in the middle of August. Although we could always count on some fog and rain, the period between the end of July and the middle of August usually promised us many sunny, warm days. The morning we took off the wind was blowing across the port quarter, and we set the sails on a broad reach on the starboard side of the boat. As I look back over our log, I see that the winds were light with no real seas. We sped over the waves to Biddeford at about five miles per hour with maximum speeds of seven miles per hour. We anchored outside of the Pool, and our anchor dragged twice, requiring us to pull it up and reset it each time. Finally, Tom and I were able to settle down and relax.

The next morning we found that the wind had shifted to the north-north/east, and the seas were building. The boat was in its element with the sails set on a close-reach on the starboard side of the boat. In our log I wrote that Casco Bay went by so quickly that we hardly saw it. We were fairly far out to sea when we passed Cape Small. We kept both the dreaded Sequin Island and the mouth of the Kennebec River on our port side, which is unusual for us. Normally we passed between them, but that day the wind and seas combined to force us to sail outside of Sequin. Then we cut north, up toward Boothbay, trimming the sails slightly as we turned the boat in a more northerly direction, slipping between Lineken Neck and Fisherman Island through the Fisherman Island Passage.

We then tacked several times, working our way up the Damariscotta River. As we approached Christmas Cove, Tom turned on the engine, and the two of us pulled in the genoa and then let the mainsail drop (see 69.557 west longitude 43.841 north latitude). We bundled it up tightly on top of the boom before calling the harbor master about getting a mooring for the night. Over the years that we have been visiting the cove, the moorings have been laid closer and closer together so that it was cramped that night, and we worried about hitting another boat. In the evening we ate dinner in a small restaurant we knew, then took a walk, and noticed that an old inn on the cove had been pulled down and construction on condominiums begun. Change was in the air.

Morning three of our passage found us on the water with little or no wind. We motor-sailed through Muscongus Bay (see 69.379 west longitude 43.929 north latitude). As I have mentioned before, any number of scenic routes through the bay exist; however, you really have to pay attention to navigating. Tom and I approached Port Clyde by passing between Allen and Thompson Islands and proceeding on to the opening between Hupper and Hart Islands, keeping Hart Island and Allen Ledge to our starboard side. We motored on past Port Clyde through the marked channel which led us into Penobscot Bay. A red-and-white whistle (R W "MP") lies just east of Mosquito Island. We used it to get our bearings and then shot almost due north to Tenant's Harbor. After visiting the general store, we sat out in the cockpit, and Tom sketched. Later we went to have lobster in the rustic harbor-side restaurant we've mentioned before; the one where they give you rocks to smash open the lobster claws.

Tom and I woke up to fog on day four of our passage. We felt we had made significant progress already towards our Bar-Harbor goal so we returned to our V-berth and went back to sleep. During the afternoon we puttered about and did chores. Tom changed *Makai's* oil and replenished the transmission fluid. And we went into the dock and got diesel and filled up the water tank. One thing about fog, the seas subside so that it was no trouble at all to dock. It was like we were on a lake.

I guess we should have seen it coming. Things were going so well. There had been no bad weather to complain until day four when we had a little fog; the seas had been with us for the most part; the winds had performed in a stellar fashion; and each day we had sailed at high speeds, almost flying across Casco, Boothbay, and Muscongus Bay on our way to Bar Harbor. We had even evaded the pain that Sequin and the mouth of the Kennebec can sometimes inflict on us. Yes, we should have seen it coming.

Day five of our passage found us up early on our way across Penobscot Bay. We sailed up through Mussel Ridge in about two hours, then crossed the western part of Penobscot and turned on the engine before rolling in the genoa and pulling in the mainsail to motor through the Fox Island Thoroughfare. Once past Vinalhaven and North Haven Islands, Tom and I let the genoa back out and released the main sheet to sail across the eastern section of Penobscot. As we approached the Deer Isle Thoroughfare, we turned the engine back on to prepare to go through the passage.

The engine sounded odd. We quickly consulted our texts and discovered that there were marine facilities on Moose Island, just west of Stonington (see again 68.678 west longitude 44.150 north latitude). We called them and explained our problem, and they directed us to motor into Allen Cove on the northern side of the Thoroughfare where they were located. I remember distinctly that I was at the wheel, and Tom had gone forward to find a mooring for us. Suddenly the engine just died. It is a sickening feeling to know you have no power and to see rocks and land all around you. I felt it go and yelled to Tom we had no engine. He quickly prepared to drop the anchor, and as we drifted back, he threw it over. I nervously watch the depth meter because this was not an anchorage we had planned, and I didn't know what kinds of depths or currents we were dealing with. Would the anchor line be long enough to hold us?

Would the current cause the anchor to drag? If it did, we had no power to enable us to reset the anchor or to maneuver in the current. We held off other boats as we informed the marine facilities of our predicament. A mechanic in a Boston Whaler quickly came along side of us. One thing I have noticed about the boating culture is that when there is a real problem, and people radio for help, others respond very quickly.

Once the mechanic arrived, he announced he would take us to a dock. I would not have thought it possible that (what seemed to me) his tiny boat could power *Makai* (a boat I call affectionately 'Baby Huey' sometimes) to the dock, but it did. Once there he examined the engine and said that this was "a first" for him – the transmission had unbolted from the back of the engine and fallen off. And there could be other problems too. With dismay we heard that it was Friday, and they could not get to work on the boat until Monday. However, they offered us a space on the dock with electricity and showers. And the town of Stonington was just a mile or so down the road. Bar Harbor had never seen further way.

SIDE BAR 10:1 SURVIVING BEING STUCK ON SHORE

Planning a passage is an exciting project that can involve the entire family. And while achieving cruise goals is important, flexibility is a key element in sailing which Tom and I have stressed throughout this text. It doesn't make sense, and may even be dangerous, to push through bad weather or the illness of a crew member just to meet a goal. And if your boat has engine troubles or blows out a sail, you simply can't go on until repairs are made. Sometimes it's just better to stop, consider, and enjoy what is around you.

Means of transportation is paramount when you are in such a predicament. Walking of course is the first option, and it can be very special to dinghy ashore and step on land. You feel like an explorer, and it is easy to imagine what early discoverers felt when they arrived on new lands. If the weather is good, the entire family can go out exploring on foot. Foggy wet weather is even enjoyable with the appropriate foul weather gear. I remember taking a refreshing hike around Harpswell Harbor in Casco Bay when in it was misty and drizzling. Although not ideal, we stretched our legs and were more relaxed when we return to the boat.

Using the dinghy to get around is an option. When we were laid up on Moose Island, we used the dinghy to go from the boat yard to the town of Stonington where we had lunch and explored. Biking is also a great idea. Either you can bring bikes on board or rent bikes where you are moored or anchored. In Provincetown we rented bikes and rode around the well-marked bike paths. They even had a bike shuttle that helped bikers explore more distant parts of the area. Gulf carts are sometimes offered at marinas where you dock or pick up a mooring. Once we took a gulf cart to go grocery shopping. Marinas sometimes make available complementary cars. We got permission to borrow one for an afternoon and drove to the nearby city of Bath to shop and mosey around the town. In Portland where we stayed at a yacht club on the south side of the harbor, the launch person took us across the harbor to a dock in the main part of the city of Portland where we spent the afternoon shopping and walking around. After dinner, we used our boat radio to call the launch and pick us up. If you end up in a mooring near a town or city, public transportation may well be available. In Portland we learned to take buses from the yacht club where we had a mooring, and in Boothbay we took a trolley around the town. There are also taxis. In one town we walked to a grocery store to restock our galley and finding our bags too heavy to lug back to the boat, we simply called a cab which took us back to the yacht club. Sailing people tend to be generous and trusting. In both Portland and Moose Island people offered us the use of their cars when they found we were having difficulties and needed to buy supplies.

A second challenge when laid up, after solving the transportation and resupplying-the-galley problems, is what to do with your days and nights. When physical exercise and exploration by foot, bike, cart, car, or bus of the area have all been tried, beach activities are an option. Although New England waters are chilly, going swimming at least for a short while is stimulating. And the region boasts of so many lovely beaches. For example, we were able to easily walk from the marina in Ebenecook, down Dogfish Head Road to Beach Road, and on to a great beach that had wonderfully-shaped boulders off of it. Shell-collecting is fun especially for children. Foraging for treats can also be rewarding. In Stage Harbor we picked mussels off of the rocks at low tide and ate them for dinner. At Ebenecook and Robinhood we hiked to places where we knew chanterelle mushrooms grew. We gathered these delicacies and added them to omelets and other dishes. At Biddeford Pool Tom and I walked along the shore and found all kinds of berry bushes, including blueberries, raspberries, and black berries, all-the-while being surrounded by the heavy scent of the rugosa roses. Bird-watching is exciting. When we were grounded in Popham Harbor by the fog, we sat for hours on the beach training our binoculars on birds with which we were unfamiliar. Looking them up in *Peterson Field Guide for Eastern Birds* which we always have on board kept our attention for hours.

In other parts of the text, we have discussed that visiting forts, museums, and art galleries may also provide enriching experiences. Dropping by the town's Chamber of Commerce, its public library, or some other public office may give you other ideas for how to explore the area.

Nights on board are special. If it isn't foggy, sitting in the cockpit and identifying the constellations can be very exciting for young people. If it is foggy and stormy, retreating to the main cabin and reading or listening to an audio-book are wonderful options. If your family is open to listening to audio-books, then sharing the stories and talking about them can be treasured experiences. I have mentioned anchoring one foggy night in Cape Neddick Harbor and listening to "The Fog Horn" by Ray Bradbury (1997, orig. 1951). The low rumble of the light-house horn made the story even more eerie and spell-binding. If you don't find audio books an option, keeping iPods charged so you can listen to music or just plain old-fashioned reading-a-book are other possibilities. I read *Moby Dick* (Melville 2012, orig. 1851) on a cruise one year. I'm not sure that I would have found it so mesmerizing if I had read it on land and at home. But there is something about being under sail and reading about Captain Ahab's quest that electrifies you, especially if you happen to see whales while underway.

Being grounded because of bad weather or engine problems can be easily reframed. Perceiving it as an opportunity to take the time to slow down and enjoy the moment must be emphasized. Sure, one can travel from Kittery, Maine to Portland in an hour. But you can also sail there in a couple of days, savoring the cool, salty breezes and anchoring at night in an unforgettable spot where blue herons soar over you to land in the shallow waters to fish. And if you are stuck in one of these spots for a little longer than anticipated, the time spent there is even more precious.

SIDE BAR 10:2 SAILING AND LIFE-LONG LEARNING

Sailing offers wonderful opportunities for all family members to learn new things. Working with maps and charts in the cockpit of a sailing vessel makes geography come alive in ways that it rarely does in the classroom. Hands-on demonstrations of the significance of latitude and longitude fix these concepts in the mind so there is no more running to the dictionary because you forgot which is which.

Everyone practices the skills associated with making inventories, organizing, and planning when sailing. Whether going on a weekend jaunt or a two-week passage, the importance of making lists of food, medicines, clothing, and other gear is made clear. You can enlist children's aid in scheduling leisure activities as well as favorite snacks so that they feel they are partners in the effort.

Sailing in New England provides many opportunities to delve into the history of the United States. On the Damariscotta River we visited the giant, 30-foot high, oyster-shell midden left by Native Americans. The Glidden Midden is thought to be over 2,000 years old. On the Isles of Shoals we discovered Native Americans used the islands as fishing camps, and on the Pemaquid peninsula we read about how the Abenaki people used the site as a major encampment.

Forts pepper the entire region, and many of them are well preserved and have enrichment programs and/or museums that families can enjoy. Fort Knox, across the river from Bucksport, Fort Popham at the entrance to the Kennebec River, Fort McClary in Pepperrell Cove, the reconstructed tower of Fort William Henry, and the archaeological site at Pemaquid all provide opportunities for families to discuss the conflicts between the English and the ex-colonists and between the early settlers of the region and the French and Native Americans.

US maritime history comes alive for life-long learners in the towns of the upper part of Penobscot Bay where premier ship-building for trade took place in the nineteenth century. Belfast, Searsport, and Castine provide marvelous opportunities for exploration of that era. In Rockport we visited the Rockport Marine Yacht Design which continues the region's long historical connection to boating. There they research, design, and build wooden boats. Bath, on the Kennebec River, has been continuously involved in shipbuilding since 1607 (Johnson 1986, 84; www.mainemartimemuseum.org). In Bath the wonderful Maine Maritime Museum covers ship building through the centuries. Evidence of the wealth this industry generated, as well as the riches that came from trade using the vessels, are apparent in the lovely homes the ship captains built and maintained. Salem, Massachusetts is a great place for young people to visit, not only because of its maritime history and the peerless Peabody Essex Museum, but because of America's infamous witch trials of the 1690s and the presence today of the fascinating Wicca movement.

On the Damariscotta River contemporary oyster-farming businesses dot the waterway (www.oysterguide.com). These "growing areas," multiplying yearly, provide the opportunity for conversations about innovative business practices as well as history-in-the-making. And in local restaurants, you can sample what is harvested from the waters.

While sailing, we discovered countless opportunities for viewing art created by New England painters or for learning about the artists themselves which allowed us to more deeply appreciate their pictures. Marsten Hartley has been classified as an American Modernist painter. He was born and grew up in Lewiston, Maine, and while he traveled abroad extensively, he called himself "the painter of Maine." On the Isles of Shoals Celia Thaxter entertained artists such as the 19th-century American Impressionist painter Frederick Childe Hassam, and on the Maple Juice Cove off the St. George's River, you can visit Christina Olson's home and grave which were made famous by the 20th-century American realist artist Andrew Wyeth in the painting, "Christina's World" (www.andrewwhyeth.com). Tom and I were able to visit Winslow Homer's studio in Prout's Neck before the Portland Art Museum took over its administration. Now you arrange to visit it through the Museum which shuttles people there (www.winslowhomer.org). Homer, America's foremost painter of the 19th-century, created fabulous pictures of the sea and the coast of Maine. Portland Art Museum exhibits his paintings as well as other American paintings on a regular basis (www.portlandmuseum.org). Tom and I never miss stopping in Portland for a day or two and visiting the Museum. Painting is not all in New England's past though. When we visited Port Clyde, Maine, we found a thriving artists' colony there with galleries that sell their works in and around the town.

Sailing has so many dimensions that it is hard to describe them all. The opportunities for learning and for developing new interests are so numerous and so rich that there is surely something there for everyone to enjoy.

That was the beginning of our five-night stay on Moose Island. Of course on Friday, Saturday, and Sunday there was no work done on the boat. Monday at 7 am a mechanic arrived and took out the transmission and adaptor plate. After a tense conference with Tom, the two were in agreement that these should be replaced. Tom also wanted new transmission cables put in. The mechanic went off to order parts. Early Tuesday morning, he was back with the new engine parts, which he inserted. Then he decided that the engine was out of alignment (by 10/1000s of an inch-whatever that means). There were also some problems with the engine mount. He returned early the next day, Wednesday, and continued to work on the engine throughout the morning. However, not only was this the fifth day on the docks, but the third day of a terrific heat wave. We were roasting out in the cockpit. Thus, since the motor was functional, we decided to stop the fine tuning and asked the mechanic to fasten the engine down so we could depart. This he did, and we paid our bill to the tune of a whopping $2,729 before leaving Moose Island.

What did we do on Saturday, Sunday, Monday, Tuesday, and half of Wednesday while this was going on? Tom and I both read a lot; Tom sketched; I caught up on our log; one day we walked to downtown Stonington which was a mile or so away; another day we went by dinghy to Stonington and shopped and ate out; we borrowed a car from someone at the marina and drove around Deer Isle; and we found a grocery store and bought provisions for the return home. Yes, the trip home, because there would be no Bar Harbor that year. The time we had allocated to explore Blue Hill Bay, Mount Desert, Frenchman Bay, and Bar Harbor had slipped away while we sat on the dock on Moose Island.

Although somewhat disappointed our passage had not turned out the way we had planned (and although the bill for fixing *Makai* stuck in our throats), Tom and I were too seasoned to let the change in plans ruin our trip. We had had a glorious sail Down East before the transmission stopped working; the weather had been superb; and the area around Moose Island where we stayed was spectacularly beautiful. One gift I was especially thankful for was that there was a heat wave while we were on the docks, rather than cold rain and fog. Five days of cold rain on a boat dock would have been intolerable.

As Tom and I left Moose Island, we talked about returning the next year and stopping by "for old times' sake." We motored across east Penobscot Bay and into Fox Islands Thoroughfare, but because it was already afternoon, we decided to anchor in Kent Cove on the north-east side of the Thoroughfare, rather than go any further. Before too long we were swimming in the cove and cooling off since the heat wave had not abated.

However, as the sun dimmed, clouds built, and the wind picked up. We were sitting in the cockpit drying off when we sensed a storm coming through. Tom quickly decided to put out a second anchor, and we turned on the motor to position the boat to accommodate it. Tom had me gently motor the boat 90 degrees to starboard of the claw anchor we already had out. Once the bow of the boat was in line with the position of the claw anchor, he dropped the Fortress anchor. We then slowly backed down, cleated the Fortress line which nudged it into position. Thus we were in a stirrup configuration with the two anchors at a 90 degree angle from one another. A good thing it was too because a real squall came at us with lightening, thunder, high winds, and frothy, churning waters. We huddled down below in the main cabin, waiting for it to pass. It was quite the tempest. Later, in Stage Harbor, we met a couple we knew, and they told us that they had been in Gosport Harbor at the Isles of Shoals when the storm blew through. They had been on a mooring, but the winds had been so strong that they were concerned that they would drag the mooring and end up on the rocks. They started the engine and powered towards the winds to reduce the pressure of the storm on the mooring line.

SIDE BAR 10:3 THUNDER AND LIGHTNING

Sailors must pay attention to the weather, and not just because they don't want a shower to spoil a pleasant afternoon, but because storms with thunder and lightning can threaten the safety of the crew and the boat. (We don't have cyclones or typhoons in New England, and hurricanes are forecast early so sailors should not be caught unawares by one while out on the water). However, thunderstorms with lightening and/or a squall line (row of thunderstorms that may stretch for 100 miles) are all too common during summers in New England.

Maloney (2003, 817-822) notes that three conditions need to be in place for the formation of a thunderstorm: (1) a lifting mechanism such as the air heating on a hot summer day, or a cold front advancing under warm air, which causes strong upward currents of air (2) instability in air currents caused by the lifting (3) moisture in the air, such as on a hot and humid day found on a mid-July afternoon in New England. He suggests that if you are out on the water on a humid day, keep an eye on the clouds. If you see cumulous clouds form and begin to pile up in the sky, be prepared to take action. What you will not be able to see as this cloud grows is that the upper part of it becomes a cirrus cloud which is composed of ice crystals and not drops of water. Once this takes place, then violent air currents will form along with a dark area in the storm cloud which is where hail and/or heavy rain are found.

Ahead of the thunderstorm come unstable and high winds, so it is a good idea to be back on your mooring, or if you are on anchor as we were in Kent Cove, put out a second anchor, when this phase hits. Gusty and shifting winds with high velocity occur as well as heavy precipitation and, perhaps, hail. Then, of course, there are sometimes lightning strikes. Maloney reviews the "30/30" rule which states that the first 30 indicates the lightening is striking 30 seconds or 6 miles away. If the time between the lightning and thunder is less than 30 counts, then stay where you are. The second 30 of the rule reminds people to wait another 30 minutes after the last lightning strike as a precaution.

In addition to being on a mooring or anchored with two anchors in a stirrup configuration, it is advisable to lower radio antennas and sails and unplug all of your electronic equipment. We have known two sailors who lost thousands of dollars' worth of electronic equipment from lightning strikes. It goes without saying you should not be in the cockpit watching the storm or out swimming, but down in the cabin where Maloney recommends that you avoid contact with any metal fittings. Depending on how bad the storm is, he also suggests that you have your life jacket on "in case you are rendered unconscious" and land in the water (p. 823).

As climate change occurs, we are having more hot and humid summers in New England. We all know the kind of muggy, sweltering day that usually ends in a thunderstorm at about 6 pm. If you are experiencing such an afternoon, it makes good sense to plan on being back at your mooring or in a solid anchorage by 4 pm.

The next day the air was clear, cool, and fresh. We proceeded through the Fox Islands Thoroughfare and across the west part of Penobscot Bay, down Mussel Ridge, past Port Clyde, to mouth of the St. George River. Tom and I chose to enter into Turkey Cove on the east side of the St. George River where we had never been. There we anchored. This cove is large, open, and protected. Our log notes that after we dropped the claw, a local sailor approached us in his dinghy and offered us the use of his mooring. Because we had already cast the anchor, we declined his offer but appreciated it. Such is the courtesy of sailors on the sea.

Tom and I continued our trip the following day, sailing past Muscongus Bay and up into Boothbay Harbor where we motored through the Townsend Gut into Ebenecook where we spent the night. We relaxed in the cockpit and watched the now familiar two parent ospreys circle around their large nest, feeding the constantly-peeping offspring they had produced.

The next morning we left Ebenecook and tried to sail down the Sheepscott River toward the mouth of the Kennebec River and Sequin Island. However, the wind was strong and on the nose of the boat. We kept the mainsail up to provide some stability but took in the genoa. As we turned southwest we were close-hauled and really working hard to get past Popham Beach at the mouth of the Kennebec. As I write this, I'm referring to the charts we used that day (plasticized to protect them). We were on a southwest tack, passing carefully-circled waypoints that had been entered into the GPS. I see red nuns, gongs, and green cans marking rocks, ledges, shoals, and other hazardous obstacles that we left behind us as we struggled past them. But as we passed between Sequin and the mouth of the Kennebec River, it really took my breath away. I once heard a famous musician say in a radio interview that he was constantly taking chances that terrified him, so after a while he realized he liked being terrified. I wouldn't exactly say that is what I felt about Sequin and the Kennebec that day, but complicated as it sounds, I was in fact scared to death, yet I wouldn't have missed it for the world.

The magnificent rocky fingers stretched out from the river's mouth and seemed far too close to *Makai* for my comfort. And the churning, frothy waters threw the boat from side to side. I am absolutely sure that if the engine had died, and the sails could not have coped with the current and winds, then we would have been lost. But nonetheless, it was so unbelievably beautiful.

Makai made it past Fuller's Rock off of Cape Small at the east end of Casco Bay, and soon we were sailing in the relative calm of the bay's islands. After Long Island, we turned north, and then southwest after Peaks Island, motor-sailing down Diamond Pass. By the time we reached Portland Harbor and picked up our mooring pick-up pole at the yacht club in south Portland, the adrenaline had stopped pumping, and I was calmer. Yet we were certainly not interested in crossing the harbor by launch and having "an urban evening." We went into the yacht club, showered with hot water, and returned to relax on board. Each night a cruise ship passed out of the harbor on its way to Yarmouth, Nova Scotia, and we loved to see it motor out with all its lights on and the people on the decks laughing and cheering. We were in bed early that night. It had been an eventful day.

The following afternoon we crossed the harbor by launch and walked up to the Portland Art Museum which was having a special exhibit on French 19th-century painters and how they depicted Paris and the countryside around the capital. The museum and the exhibit were lovely, and we happily spent the afternoon there. We stopped for raw oysters in a restaurant on the way back to the boat.

The last night of our cruise we spent in Stage Harbor, one of our favorite spots. I brought us through the lobster-infested entrance, and Tom found us a nice anchorage where we dropped the hook. Friends of ours were anchored nearby, and we swapped stories about how we made it through the storm that we experienced while in Kent Cove. They were the ones who had problems in Gosport Harbor that night. Later we went to the beach and swam, and then we had a nice dinner. As the sun set, an incredibly-orange and huge moon began to rise over the horizon. We sat in the cockpit, struck with awe, at this breathtaking sight and agreed that we would not easily forget that evening.

On our final cruise day, the seas were flat and the wind light. We had a comfortable trip to Pepperrell Cove where we picked up our mooring. Not wanting the cruise to be over yet, we took our time puttering around the boat and gathering things together to take home. As we shut down our equipment and arranged the sail cover on the mainsail, the laughing gulls and terns swooped around us. We took extra care to place the tarpaulin over the dodger and mainsail to protect it from their droppings. Finally, we studied our list of things we had to do before leaving *Makai* alone on her mooring. Everything was accounted for so there was nothing left to do but load up the dinghy and head for the dock.

Our passage had been, as usual, a unique experience like no other. We had made plans, and some of them worked out while others had not. We had not expected the solitary beauty of Kent Cove or the moon over Stage Harbor or the splendor of Sequin. Nor had we anticipated having to cope with our transmission dying on us. In all, it was as we had learned to expect-- from cruising off the coast of New England. One surprise after another.

Chapter Eleven

You and Sailing

The Meaning of Sailing to You

Tom and I sat in the cockpit one night in Pepperrell Cove, talking about our sailing experiences. What did they mean to us? What had we learned from them? By the end of the evening, we had come up with several ideas. These could be relevant to individuals, couples working together as we did, or families with children.

Freedom-with-responsibility was the first concept that Tom spontaneously thought of. He said that he experienced such a feeling of joy when he was able to leave the petty concerns of work behind him and step onto the boat. On board, more fundamental concerns occupied his mind. Taking care of the boat, and of yourself and your crew, become paramount. Also, although you can't affect the winds, sea, fog, and rocks that threaten your security, you have direct control over the boat and any of the decisions made about it, and indirectly over yourself and your passengers. Things are clearer out there on the water. On one hand, no one is telling you what to do, but, on the other hand, you can't blame others for mistakes you make.

A second related concept has to do with "sailing-as-a-trial," a test to see if you have the knowledge, strength, and fortitude to endure. I suspect this will sound a little philosophical, but let me quote Joseph Conrad's *Youth*. For some people, possibly Tom, sailing is "the endeavor, the test, the trial of life" (Conrad 1903, p. 12). You have to remember that Tom did blue-water sailing, taking on the Atlantic on a 40-foot boot when he was 30. My experiences were far less grand, but I got a glimpse of what this idea meant, in a small way, when we were off Wood Island, trying to make it into Biddeford. You may recall the engine overheated, and I had to sail up to Richmond Island and Seal Cove while Tom tried to cope with the engine.

SIDE BAR 11:1 OVERHEATING OF THE AUXILIARY ENGINE

If your sailboat has an auxiliary engine, it is important that it functions properly when needed. Engines, whether fueled by gasoline or diesel fuel, produce a lot of heat since they are combusting fuel to develop power. Essential in all such engines is the system to cool the core and exhaust to a manageable temperature.

In the case of outboard engines, the cooling system is completely housed in the engine. Raw water (fresh or salt) is pumped through an opening in the lower shaft of the engine. Screening devices are used to prevent dirt and debris from entering the engine. The water then circulates through the engine and is expelled, usually through a hose near the top of the engine. Should the outboard engine run abnormally or irregularly, check to verify that water is passing out through the hose. If not, slowly power the engine down and shut it off. Consult your manuals to see if you can access the areas where an obstruction to the water intake or filter may exist.

In the case of inboard engines, usually a temperature gauge and an alarm sounds, should operating temperatures significantly exceed specifications. Inboard engines get their water through a through-hull fitting covered by a strainer. *If your boat's raw-water-intake does not have a strainer, replace the through-hull fitting with one that has a strainer.* We learned this when anchored in Benner Bay, St. Thomas V.I. the sea grass capital of the world. Strainers prevent large debris from entering the cooling system. The through-hull fitting is usually connected to a stopcock or valve inside the boat that can be closed to stop water from entering the system. *Know where this fitting is and how to access it.* Beyond the stopcock is the raw-water-filter. Usually it is made of transparent material which allows you to see any debris in the filter. It should be easy to disassemble, allowing you to clear all obstructions. Reassemble the filter, open the stopcock, check for leaks and restart your engine. Hopefully while you are performing these acts, someone competent has managed to keep the craft from harm using the sails to provide helm, if necessary.

I can safely say that of the two of us, I had the better job. Tom was definitely not having a good time. He was down below where the tossing-and-turning of the boat was magnified, trying to take the companionway apart so he could access the engine, standing nearly upside down, so that he could diagnose what was wrong with the engine and fix it. All of this without adequate light. He then came into the cockpit and took everything out of the starboard sail locker, secured the hatch open, and squeezed into the locker to access the raw-water-intake filter. When he got into the locker, he found the filter clogged with grasses and debris. He then shut off the raw-water seacock and tried to take apart the filter. But, ultimately, the sea conditions made it impossible to fix.

While all this was going on, I was in the cockpit, in the fresh air, and had a great view. However, I was alone; I was responsible for sails which were going every-which-way; the seas were stormy; the air was cold; and I just wanted to get into Wood Island Harbor and have a nice hot cup of coffee. At one point I went to the hatch way and pleaded with Tom to turn on the engine and make a run for Wood Island, but he was adamant. That would destroy the engine, and for what? We were in no danger. "Sail," he said ominously. I returned to the wheel, and feeling a bit like someone under the command of Captain Ahab in *Moby Dick*, I sailed.

The hours went by (yes, hours), and Tom was still in the sail locker, and I continued to contend with the choppy seas and gusty wind as I sailed northeast. We sailed across Saco Bay, but I scarcely noticed Old Orchard Beach in the distance. We also passed Prout's Neck where we had visited Homer's studio one foggy day. Then we approached Richmond Island Harbor and Seal Cove on the other side of the island, just southwest of Cape Elizabeth. I steered the *Makai* towards Seal Cove, and the sails remained full, although not as trim as I would have liked. The closer we got, the less choppy the seas and the quieter the winds. Finally, we serenely sailed into the cove.

Tom came up for air and to see what was happening. We pulled in the genoa, and he went forward and prepared to drop the anchor. Even without engine power, we managed to tuck *Makai* into a tranquil spot and drop the anchor before the boat stopped. I was extremely proud of myself. I had sailed the boat for hours with no help or advice, and I had gotten us into safe haven. Not the stuff that *The Old Man and the Sea* describes perhaps, but none-the-less I felt I had learned something important about endurance (and about sailing of course).

Added to the list of what sailing means to Tom and me is a new respect, even reverence, for the seas, winds, waves, rocks, and shoreline.

Being outdoors all day is special if you have an office job where you are indoors a lot of the time. The fresh air, the sun, and even the fog are experienced differently than when in your normal home routine. Basking in the sun, walking trails, sitting on the beach, and of course being on the water in a boat alter your point of view about what is important, healthy, and beautiful. And Seguin? The terrible but magnificent Sequin, well – I stand in awe of it. Sailing provides those special and unforgettable moments that stay with you forever.

Sailing is also adventure. For how many thousands of year and in how many countries has sailing been synonymous with exploration? In Conrad's *Youth*, the author describes his first voyage as second mate. It was his first voyage East, and even after countless disasters, including the burning of the ship and the crew's flight to three lifeboats, his resolve to get to the East never wavered. Finally, after days in an open dinghy, the second mate and the few men with him approached an unknown harbor in the East. Conrad writes in his usual unforgettable style,

> "And this is how I see the East. I have seen its secret places and have looked into its very soul; but now I see it always from a small boat, a high outline of mountains, blue and afar in the morning; like faint mist at noon; a jagged wall of purple at sunset….And I see a bay, a wide bay, smooth as glass and polished like ice, shimmering in the dark….suddenly, a puff of wind, a puff faint and tepid and laden with strange odours of blossoms, of aromatic wood, comes out of the still night-the first sigh of the East on my face. That I can never forget. It was impalpable and enslaving, like a charm, like a whispering promise of mysterious delight (Conrad 1903, p. 37)."

I've never had to flee a burning ship, and neither has Tom. But I have sailed into unknown harbors, and so has Tom, although his experiences Have been a bit more exotic than mine, including the Azores, Gibraltar, Tortola, and England. There is something about coming ashore in a place you don't know that makes it a special experience. When I think back on taking the dinghy into the marina on the island of Southport, it was a unique experience to discover little coves and beaches and cottages with lovely gardens on foot. It was quite different than driving around and seeing places almost fly by.

Another more practical aspect of sailing has to do with problem-solving. This overlaps to a certain extent with acquiring new knowledge and skills, such as learning how to trim a sail or chart a course. (See Side Bar 10:2 Life-Long Learning.) However, it is something different than that also. When something goes wrong, you have to think on your feet and find alternative ways to do things. (See Side Bar 9:1 Hot Wiring Your Engine.) This is obviously something important that children can be taught in families early in life. When they attempt new ways of doing things, are they supported by other family members, or are they made fun of or discounted? Also in man-woman couples, especially in a situation like Tom and mine where Tom knew so much more about sailing than I did, the one who knows less needs to feel like their efforts are respected. I know I always felt that Tom appreciated my efforts and never once, in all our years of boating, did he make fun of me or get angry at me when I did something dumb (even when I let the halyard go to the top of *Northstar* – although he was close to saying something biting, I'm sure.)

Another characteristic of the sailing lifestyle is that it opens new dimensions for you, ones that you didn't even know about. Sailing was absolutely new for me, and yet, over a twenty-five year period, I learned a lot about it, and I really loved it. Some of the related skills, such as math, chart reading, and the use of technology, I already had, but with sailing, I applied these skills differently, thus strengthening them. I also enjoyed art appreciation before I learned to sail, but with sailing, I discovered new painters and subject matter. I wonder how many special art exhibitions we attended at the Portland Art Museum? And then there was Christina Olson's home on the St. George River where Andrew Wyeth painted, and Prout's Neck where Homer had his studio. Jamie Wyeth's studio-lighthouse off of Tenant's Harbor also comes to mind. All of these are now linked by sailing. Bird watching was totally new to me too. And I first came to enjoy it while under sail, and I brought that hobby back to land with me where I enjoy it today. This list could go on, and I suspect other sailors could share their own equally-long versions with you.

Resources for Continuing Your Sailing Progress

Once you commit yourself to learning to sail, you might wonder how to proceed. Don't discount "how to" books as you begin to learn about it in a hands-on fashion. Once you begin to formally or informally take lessons, reading about it reinforces what you are learning and helps you to remember vocabulary and concepts. The "For Dummies" series has a helpful book about sailing by J. J. Isler and Peter Isler (2006) which is nicely written for novices and for those who want a refresher book. It lists as its outcomes – go to a sailing school; launch a boat and sail; learn to navigate, anchor, and dock; charter a boat or enter a race; choose and care for a boat.

The American Sailing Association has two volumes that I found helpful. Their introductory text (2010) clearly introduces you to boats, sails, and fundamental skills, while their book on coastal cruising (2012) provides more in depth learning about sail trim, navigation, motors, and seamanship. One thing that I like about their approach is that it is organized by clear-cut, two-page lessons, so that you feel like you are progressing through a course as you go through the book. I keep these two books on board.

Steve Sleight's works (2001, 2011) on sailing take the new boater from first stepping into a boat, then learning the basics and improving boating skills, and finally to cruising and navigating. He also has great diagrams and figures showing you how to, for example, right a dinghy.

Local yacht clubs can be resources and/or provide sailing lessons for children and adults. You can research these easily by Googling "yacht club sailing lessons," or some similar phrase. Web pages provide descriptions of the schools, who they service, when the classes take place, and applications. You can also email leaders of the schools, or phone them for more information. For example, when we sailed down to Newburyport, Massachusetts on the Merrimac River in *Northstar*, we stayed at the American Yacht Club. As soon as we walked into the place, we felt that there was a lot of positive energy. People were rushing around to prepare for a race out on the river, and other scheduled events were posted on boards around the club. We discovered that they have summer sailing programs for children from ten to 18 years of age. There are 15 students per class, so they attempt to keep the size of the classes small. The Kittery Point Maine Yacht Club near where we summer also offers sailing lessons in small boats for junior and adult sailors.

One caveat. If you are the parent of a pre-teen daughter, and you want her to take sailing lessons, as was my sister's case, you may want to discuss with the instructor how they handle teaching girls and boys in coed classes. Unfortunately, sometimes instructions take place in small boats where they place a boy and a girl. The boy takes over, while the girl shyly holds back, thus missing out on the learning experience. If there are boy-girl teams in the yacht club that you choose, try to ensure that the instructor will make certain that the girls are provided with the space to learn too.

Sailing lessons or even schools are not only available at yacht clubs. You can find them just about everywhere, but especially in coastal areas. The American Sailing Association's web page helps get people in touch with sailing schools all over the United States. There even special schools for women. (See Side Bar 11:1.)

SIDE BAR 11:2 SAILING SCHOOLS

Many people learn to sail with their families or with friends who happen to have boats. However, sometimes that doesn't happen or it isn't enough for the individual who wants more formal instruction. Luckily there are a many resources for people to choose from.

If you Google "sailing schools," any number of web pages come up for you to investigate in wonderful-sounding places like sunny San Diego, California and the tropical Virgin Islands. If, like me, you want to more information about their reputation and about the quality of instruction you receive from them, then I suggest you visit the web site of the American Sailing Association (ASA) (http://www.asa.com/sailing-schools.html). They have comprehensive lists of learning opportunities in nearly every state. They also offer their own classes which are taught to ASA Standards, recognized worldwide as been both safe and thorough.

Their web pages make clear that you should earn sailing certification if you plan on sailing a keelboat such as *Northstar* or *Makai*. ASA sailing certification has been approved by the US Coast Guard and qualifies you to charter boats internationally. It offers a variety of sailing certification programs including keelboat, small boat, and multihull boat sailing. In addition to these major certification programs, the ASA provides standards for more specific activities such as docking and radar use. Certification requires students to demonstrate both knowledge and skill competencies which instructors evaluate using written and actual on-the-water tests. To take other more advanced courses, they suggest practicing from 24 to 40 hours on what you just learned before enrolling in the next more complex course.

They offer ASA101 Basic Keelboat Sailing which takes place on a 20 to 27 foot sailboat in light to moderate winds and seas. You learn about the parts and functions of a boat, helm commands, basic sail trim, buoyage, etc. ASA103 Basic Coastal Cruising requires ASA101 Basic Keelboat Sailing Certification. The goal in AS103 is "to demonstrate your ability to skipper a sloop-rigged auxiliary powered keelboat" of about 25 to 35 feet in length in moderate winds and sea conditions. Cruising sailboat vocabulary, boat systems, engine operations, docking, sail trim, navigation, anchoring, safety, etc. are taught. By the time you enroll in ASA106 Advanced Coastal Cruising, certification is required in not only Basic Keelboat Sailing and Basic Coastal Cruising, but in Bareboat Chartering and Coastal Navigation. ASA106 sounds formidable in that students work with large sailboats, between 30 and 50 feet in both the day- and nighttime, in coastal and inland waters, and in any kind of weather (http://www.asa.com/lts-asa-standards-summary.html). The movie, *The Perfect Storm*, came to mind when I uneasily read about "any kind of weather."

Being a woman and coming to sailing as an adult and not a child, I noticed that there were several web sites that catered to women or to couples. An excellent all-round web site belongs to the National Women's Sailing Association (www.womensailing.org). On its home page, it states that its mission is "dedicated to enriching the lives of women and girls through education and access to the sport of sailing." They have a newsletter called "Take the Helm," and they organize conferences and other activities. *Women Under Sail* operates in Casco Maine and specializes in instruction for women who are beginners or operating at the intermediate level (www.womenundersail.com). Instruction takes place in three days on a 44-foot ketch. I read through some of the reviews which were favorable and heartfelt. *The Steve and Doris Colgate Offshore Sailing School* lists campuses in Captiva and Ft. Meyers Beach, Florida; in St. Michaels, Maryland; and in the British Virgin Islands (www.offshoresailing.com/sailing-courses/girlfriend-getaways.aspx). They state they can customize sailing lessons for women in groups of four or more. *Ladyship Sailing* bills itself as ASA approved (www.ladyshipsailing.com). They offer sailing courses for women and for couples, describing on their web pages courses such as "Tooltime for Ladies" and "3 Days Learn to Sail Certification."

It is amazing how many resources there are out there, and how available and relatively inexpensive they are. In fact you can easily combine a vacation with one of the courses in a sailing school such as those in Florida or the Virgin Islands. However, I must add the disclaimer that I have no personal experience with any of them, and you should research each of them carefully before committing your life, time, and money to them.

Another way to develop your sailing skills is to read and contribute to sailing blogs. One that I found at www.sailblog.com helps sailors to find boats, view photos and text posted by others, provide maps which describe where members of the blogs are (this is a comprehensive map built on Google Earth), and facilitate the functioning of a community of sailors. I started to read postings and found it hard to stop. "Zipee Too" from Humber Yawl Club, which, I discovered, is in northeast England, regularly blogged while on their cruise off of Sweden. They were slowly working their way through the Swedish archipelago, finding gorgeous anchorages. Sue and Howard on their 39-foot Oyster hailed from Ipswich in southern England. They were on cruise too, traveling from the Channel Islands to France where they visited Boulogne and Calais. It's these kinds of blogs that make us dream.

Reading fiction, biographies, and autobiographies about sailing is also helpful. Books not only give you ideas about sailing better or sailing destinations, but they can also provide you with topics to discuss with other sailing *aficionados*.

SIDE BAR 11:3 ANNOTATED READING LIST

On sailing trips, there is time to slow down and enjoy things like conversation, nature, and reading. On a rainy lay-over day, I revel in curling up on a bunk with a cup of coffee and reading for the afternoon. I suspect each sailor has their favorite list of books. Here are some of mine. Several of them are "oldies," and some are obscure, which makes them extra special.

Aebi, T. 2005. *I've Been Around.* Sheridan House. This is a collection of essays written by a woman who circumnavigated the globe when she was eighteen (see below entry). She combines sailing stories from trips she has taken all over the world with lessons for living her life. For example she writes about how we need to be resourceful and inventive when we face the challenges of daily life.

Aebi, T. 1989. *Maiden Voyage: The First American Woman – and the Youngest Person Ever-to Circumnavigate the Globe Alone.* New York: Ballantine Books. This case caused quite a sensation in the 1980s when a father reportedly asked his daughter to choose between a college education and a sailboat. She chose the sailboat and somehow also accepted a challenge to sail around the world. It is an extraordinary story filled with exotic episodes and real bravery.

Caswell, C. (ed.). 2004. *The Greatest Sailing Stories Ever Told: Twenty-seven Unforgettable Stories.* Lyons Press. This is a fun book to dip into once in a while.

Dana, R. H. 1947 (orig. 1841). *Two Years Before the Mast.* Norwalk, CT: The Heritage Press. The account of how Dana contracted measles while at Harvard and took time off from college to spend two years as a foremast hand is now famous. He traveled on board the *Pilgrim* around the Cape Horn to California. Then he returned to Boston on the *Alert.* His unvarnished account documents the brutality of the sailor's life, and when he returned to Boston he worked to improve their lot.

Gowdey, D. 1994. *Before the Wind: True Stories About Sailing.* International Marine/Ragged Mountain Press. This is a collection of 25 sailing stories, interviews, poems, including one from Joshua Slocum, the first man to sail around the world alone (see entry below), and from Robert Louis Stevenson, who made a passage to North America.

MacArthur, E. 2003. *Taking on the World: A Sailor's Extraordinary Solo Race Around the World.* International Marine/Ragged Mountain Press. In 2001 MacArthur made international headlines when she, at 24 years of age, placed second in the grueling Vendee-Globe race. The book sketches her life before telling the story of her 94-day voyage.

Manry, R. 1965. *Tinkerbelle.* Harper and Row. A forty-seven year old man sailed from Falmouth, Massachusetts to Falmouth, England alone in a tiny thirteen and a half foot sloop. It is thought to be the smallest boat to ever do such a crossing. It took Manry 70 days. He said that he believed the *Tinkerbelle* managed the crossing because it was watertight with the hatches closed; it was unsinkable; and it had a self-righting ability.

Melville, H. 1979 (orig. 1851). *Moby Dick*. Franklin Center, Pennsylvania: The Franklin Library. This is the quintessential sailing book that you may not have read in school because of its size. I took it along on a sailing cruise Down East one year and read it, not as a complex piece of literature, but as a great adventure story. I was riveted by Melville's rich description of life on nineteenth-century sailing boats. Some of his accounts border on the technical. For example, there are numerous chapters explaining how whales are killed and dismembered. But overall there is a great deal of energy and a surprising amount of humor in the book.

Moyes, P. 1961. *Down Among the Dead Men*. New York: Holt, Rinehart, and Winston. This murder mystery is set in what I assume is a fictional town named Berrybridge Haven which lies east of London on the banks of the Berry River about four miles from the North Sea. A police inspector and his wife join another couple who own a sailboat that is moored in the Berry River for a sailing holiday. The murder mystery is fun of course, but the first sixty pages or so of the book do a fine job in explaining boats and sailing.

Slocum, J. 1956 (orig. 1900). *Sailing Alone Around the World*. New York: Dover Publications, Inc. This is another sailing classic that was written in the nineteenth century by a New England sea captain who sailed around the world alone in his 34-foot boat named *Spray*. Unlike Tania Aebi, he had considerable sailing experience before his three-year voyage; nonetheless he was challenged in places like southern South America where he was blown off course and forced to pass through the Strait of Magellan, not once, but twice, even as he beat off indigenous raiders who tried to board his boat.

Snow, C.P. 2000 (orig. 1932.) Cornwall, United Kingdom: House of Stratus. *Death Under Sail*. The first part of this book describes how a group of English friends join together for a sailing holiday in the Broads, which are part of the fen country off the North Sea in central-east England. A murder occurs while they on board, so the police soon ground them in a town. However, before that, Snow describes the boat and what sailing is like on the Broads.

White, R. 1985. *Two on an Island: A Memory of Marina Cay*. New York: W. W. Norton & Company. Back in the 1980s when Tom and I were spending time each winter in the Virgin Islands, I found a wonderful memoir of a man and his wife who in the 1930s bought a tiny island off of Tortola, named Marina Cay, where they built a concrete house and cistern and lived for several years. To get to and from Road Town, the capital of Tortola where they shopped and did errands, they sailed a small sailboat. One of the more memorable parts of the book is when the wife's mother comes to visit. They pick her up one evening in the middle of a storm and decide to try to make it home to their island despite stormy seas and sheets of rain. It was quite a trip.

You can subscribe to any number of sailing magazines. Google "sailing magazines" or something like that, but here are a few suggestions. *The Sailing Magazine* is a helpful general magazine, while *Blue Water Sailing Magazine* focuses on ocean sailing, and *Sailing World* emphasizes racing, gear, expert advice, and events.

Once engaged with the sailing lifestyle, there is no end of ways you can develop your skills. It is a broad field that accommodates everyone's interests, no matter how unique you feel yours might be.

Terms I Learned

A

Aft – at the stern

Aft cabin – cabin near stern of the boat

Anti-fouling – a compound applied to the lower part of the hull that discourages the growth of marine life

B

Backstay – a stay leading from the top of the mast to the stern of the boat.

Beat into the wind – sailing with the wind just off the nose (bow) of the boat. (See also sailing against the wind.)

Bell – navigational marker.

Bilge – the bottom of the boat; the lower part of the ship's hold.

Blocks – pulleys through which sheets and halyards are routed.

Blue water sailing – ocean sailing where you are out of sight of land. The boat normally keeps sailing day and night. If there are teams of people on board, then they take turns sleeping. If there is only one person on board, as there was for example in Slocum's *Sailing Alone Around the World* (see Reading List), then either the tiller is tied off or the boat is put on auto pilot while the person sleeps. (Contrast with coastal sailing. See below.)

Boom – a long pole extending from the mast back to hold the foot (the bottom) of the mainsail stretched out.

Bow – front of the boat.

Bulkhead – one of the partitions that divides the inside of a boat into compartments and that provides structural support.

Burgee – a small triangular flag that flies from the mast identifying the yacht club to which the boat belongs.

C

Can - a green (formerly black) cylindrical-shaped marker showing one side of a navigational channel. Opposite of it is usually a nun (see below).

Centerboard – movable keel that is lowered through a slot in the floor of a sailboat which provides stability and reduces leeway. Centerboards facilitate sailing in shallow waters where deep keels might impede the boat.

Cleat – a piece of secured metal or wood to which ropes can be tied.

Close-hauled – sailing as close to the wind as possible. Sails are set tightly flat.

Coastal sailing – sailing within sight of land. Usually you stop each night. (Contrast this with blue water sailing. See above.)

Come about – turning the boat so that the bow passes through the oncoming wind. The sails move to the opposite side of the boat. Synonymous with tack.

Companionway – stairway or ladder that leads from the cockpit to the cabin of the boat.

D

Displacement – the weight of the water displaced by a floating boat which is the weight of the boat.

Dodger – canvas stretched across the companionway and part of the cockpit which protects the crew from spray and wind

Draft – the depth of water occupied by a boat calculated by measuring the distance between the waterline and the lowest point of the keel

E

Ebb tide- the tide flows out; going from high to low water. (Contrast with flood tide.)

F

Flood tide- the tide flows in; going from low water to high. (Contrast with ebb tide.)

Fo'c'sle or Forecastle – the section of a boat below deck located forward of the foremast.

Following sea- sea traveling in the same direction as the boat. (Contrast with head sea.)

Foot – the bottom edge of the sail

Forestay – a stay leading from the top of the mast to the bow of the boat.

Furl – to roll up a sail and fasten it to a pole.

G

Galley – the kitchen of a yacht.

Genoa – a large forward sail which overlaps with the mainsail when both are out.

Gong - navigational marker.

GPS – Global Positioning System – user-friendly technology that depends on satellites to determine latitude and longitude. Its first widespread military use was in the Desert Storm War. Then it spread into the general population and is now widely used by boaters, archaeologists, geologists, and car owners.

Gunk holing – a kind of cruise where you move from attractive anchorage to anchorage spending a lot of time exploring.

H

Halyard – the rope you use to pull up the sail.

Hawseholes – holes in the bow for the mooring or anchoring lines.

Head – water closet; the space where the toilet is located.

Headsail – a sail such as the jib or spinnaker which is set ahead of the mainsail.

Head sea – sea traveling in the opposite direction to the boat. (Contrast with following sea.)

Heel- to lean over.

Helm – steering pole or wheel.

Hull – the body of a boat from the rail down, excluding the engine.

I

Involuntary jibe – (definitely something to prevent); when the sails and boom shift from one side of the boat to the other without the crew being prepared; the boom can cause damage to the boat if the wind is strong enough.

J

Jib – a sail secured forward of the mast.

Jibe – to shift the mainsail from one side of the boat to the other, turning the boat so that the stern passes through the wind. The sails move to the opposite side of the boat. This maneuver requires great care in anything but light winds. (I definitely learned the power of the jibe in 1989 on our way through the New Jersey Intercoastal Waterway. We were sailing with the wind behind us, jibing back and forth through some mud flats. I had the wheel at one point and jibed too quickly so that the boom thudded from one side of the boat to the other. The entire boat shook in a very frightening way.)

K

Kedge- moving a boat by deploying a small anchor, in addition to a main anchor, and pulling on it.

Keel – the extension of the hull that provides stability for the boat and that reduces leeway.

Ketch - a sailboat with two masts; the second smaller one lies forward of the rudder. (Contrast with yawl.)

Knot – the speed of one nautical mile (1.15 miles) per hour. (See nautical mile.)

L

Land breeze – wind from the land; usually happens at night and in the early morning when the land has cooled off more than the sea. The relatively warmer sea air rises, and then the cooler land breeze moves in under it.

Latitude – distance in degrees north and south of the equator.

Lee side - downwind side of a boat

Leeward – downwind of something; blowing with the wind. (Contrast with windward.)

Longitude – distance in degrees east and west of the Greenwich Meridian (zero degrees).

Loran – a navigation system that was popular in the 1980s. It depended on radio signals to determine latitude and longitude.

Luff – the forward edge of the sail.

Luff (to luff) – when the sail loosely flaps.

M

Mainsheet – a rope that secures the boom in the appropriate position to maximize wind thrust for the desired course.

Mast – the vertical pole that supports the mainsail.

Mooring – a structure to which a boat can be secured while in the water; in the *Makai's* case, there is a 5,000 pound block of granite in Pepperrell Cove, Maine. A chain binds the block to a large plastic identifying ball (aptly called a mooring ball) which floats on the surface of the water. Lines (ropes) are attached to this ball. We use a pick-up pole to pick up these lines and secure them to cleats on deck, thus securing the boat to the granite block.

N

Nautical mile – 1.15 miles

Nun – a red conical marker showing one side of a navigational channel. Opposite of it is usually a green can. It can also mark a navigational hazard.

P

Passage-boat trip.

Port – the left hand side of the boat when you face the bow.

Preventer – a rope that secures the boom so as to mitigate against involuntary jibing. It can also adjust sail curvature to improve efficiency.

Pulpit – the extended, railed platform jutting out from the bow.

R

Rail – edge of the deck where it meets the hull. It is usually slightly raised and supports the stanchions and lifelines.

Reach – to sail with the wind on the beam.

Reef the sail – reduce the size of the sail by taking in part of it.

Rode – the rope and/or chain between the boat and the anchor.

Roller furling – a mechanism that rolls the genoa up and secures it at the bow of the boat. *Trull II* did not have roller furling, so Tom had to go to the bow of the boat and pull the sail up or let it down from there. *Makai* has roller furling so the genoa can be adjusted from the cockpit of the boat – something we much appreciate when the seas are rough.

Rudder-a movable underwater section at the stern of the boat used for steering.

Run before the wind – sail with the wind just off the stern of the boat. (See sail with the wind behind you.)

S

Safety harness- a harness attached to a line that is secured to the boat and worn by crew members in bad weather.

Sail against the wind (also beat into the wind)– if you think about the directions from which the wind can come to be a clock, then imagine that the wind coming from 10, 11, 1 or 2 o'clock. There is a sense of movement and speed when compared to sailing with the wind behind you.

Sail on a beam reach - if you think about the directions from which the wind can come to be a clock, then imagine that the wind coming from 3 or 9 o'clock.

Sail with the wind behind you (also run before the wind) – if you think about the directions from which the wind come to be a clock, then imagine the wind coming from 7, 8, 4, or 5 o'clock. When you run, there is the sense you are not moving very fast even though you might be. It is also a warmer trip in places like New England where the wind can be brisk if you are beating.

Schooner – a boat with two or more masts; unlike ketches and yawls, the second mast is not considerably smaller than the main mast.

Sea breeze – the wind blowing from the sea; it usually occurs during the day when the air over the land is hotter and rises, and the cooler sea wind blows in under it.

Sheet – the rope you use to pull in the sail or to let it out. A jib or genoa has two sheets – one to pull the sail to the starboard side, and one to pull it to the port side. *North Star's* sheets were colored green and red. The red one was on the port side (I remembered this by associating it in my mind with red port wine), while the green was on the starboard side.

Shoal – shallow area

Sloop – a kind of sailboat that has one mast. All of Tom's boats have been sloops.

Spinnaker – large light sail used in light winds. The top of the sail is run up the forward stay, and one of the ends at the bottom of the sail is attached to a long pole (called a spinnaker pole) and the other end to a sheet. Many times these sails are brightly colored.

Spring lines – lines from about midship aft and forward where they are secured on the dock to prevent the boat from surging backwards or forwards.

Starboard – the right hand side of the boat when you are facing the bow.

Stern – the back of the boat.

T

Tack - turning the boat so that the bow passes through the oncoming wind. The sails move to the opposite side of the boat. Synonymous with come about.

Tell-tales – small lengths of material attached to both sides of the sail which give information about air flow over the sail.

Tiller – a handle for turning the boat's rudder and thus steering the boat. *North Star* had a tiller, but *Makai* has a wheel. (See wheel.)

Topping lift – ropes that pull the boom up and out of the way when there are no sails up. In *Down Among the Dead Men*, Moyes (see Reading List) mentions that in England such a device is called a boom gallows.

It sits behind the cockpit, and the boom rests in it until sails are hoisted up, lifting the boom out of this cradle.

Trim- to adjust the set of a sail.

Turning the boat into the wind – situate the boat so it is directly facing the wind, thus allowing the sails to flap freely. Boats are normally turned into the wind when sails are hoisted or taken down.

W

Weigh anchor-to lift the anchor off the bottom.

Wheel – a wheel for turning the boat's rudder and thus steering the boat. *Makai* has a wheel.

Whistle - navigational marker.

Winch-a hand-operated or powered machine for hauling in sheets, halyards or anchor ropes. *Makai* has hand-operated winches to bring in the genoa and mainsail, and an electrically-powered winch to weigh the anchor.

Windlass-winch used to raise the anchor.

Windward – the direction from which the wind is blowing; blowing into the wind. (Contrast with leeward.)

Y

Yawl – a sailboat with two masts; the second smaller one lies aft of the rudder. (Contrast with ketch.)

References Cited

American Sailing Association. 2010. *The American Sailing Association's Sailing Made Easy*. Los Angeles, CA: American Sailing Association.

American Sailing Association. 2012. *The American Sailing Association's Coastal Cruising Made Easy*. Los Angeles, CA: American Sailing Association.

Bradbury, Ray. 1997 (orig. 1951). *The Fog Horn*. SRA/McGraw-Hill Publishing Company.

Eaton, Jonathan. 2013. *Chapman Piloting, Seamanship, and Small Boat Handling*. 67th Edition. New York: Hearst Books.

Husick, Charles. 2009. *Chapman Piloting, Seamanship, and Small Boat Handling*. 66th Edition. New York: Hearst Books.

Cantrell, Debra. 2001. *Changing Course: A Woman's Guide to Choosing the Cruising Life*. Camden, ME: International Marine/McGraw-Hill Companies.

Colgate, Doris. 1999. *Sailing: A Woman's Guide*. Camden, ME: Ragged Mountain Press/McGraw-Hill Company.

Colgate, Steve and Doris, Colgate. 2009. *Fast Track to Sailing: Learn to Sail in Three Days*. Camden, ME: International Marine/McGraw-Hill Company.

Conrad, Joseph. 1903. *Youth*. Garden City, NY: Doubleday, Doran, and Company.

Isler, J. J. and Peter Isler. 2006. *Sailing For Dummies*. Second Edition. Holboken, NJ: Wiley Publishing, Inc.

Johnson, Don. 1986. *Cruising Guide to Maine: Volume I Kittery to Rockland*. Stamford, CT: Wescott Cove Publishing Company.

Johnson, Don. 1987. *Cruising Guide to Maine: Volume II Rockport to Eastport*. Stamford, CT: Wescott Cove Publishing Company.

MAPTECH Embassy Guides. 1999. *Maine Coast: Coverage from Kittery to the Canadian Border*. First Edition. Andover, MA: MAPTECH, INC.

MAPTECH 2010. Embassy Cruising Guide: New England Coast. 9th Edition. New Bedford, MA: MAPTECH.

Melville, Herman. 2012 (orig. 1851). *Moby Dick*. NY: Createspace Independent Publishing Platform, Signet Classic Edition.

Putz, George. 1985. *The Maine Coast*. Edison, NJ: Chartwell Books, Inc.

Sleight, Steve. 2001. *KISS (Keep It Simple Series) Guide to Sailing*. New York: DK Publishing Inc.

Sleight, Steve. 2011. *The Complete Sailing Manual*. 3rd Edition. NY: DK Publishing.

Taft, Hank, Jan Taft, and Curtis Rindlaub. 1996. *A Cruising Guide to the Maine Coast*. Third Edition. Peaks Island, ME: Diamond Pass Publishing, Inc.

Taft, Hank, Jan Taft, and Curtis Rindlaub. 2008. *A Cruising Guide to the Maine Coast*. Fifth Edition. Peaks Island, ME: Diamond Pass Publishing, Inc.

Biographies

Over twenty-five years ago, Debra Picchi joined Tom Desrosiers on his sailboat at a New Hampshire marina for an afternoon sail. This led to her crewing for him on various sailboats as she learned to sail herself during the years that followed. A cultural anthropologist by profession, she brings several of her skills to bear on this project. She is an educator and a writer who has taught at the university level and has published many scholarly articles and two editions of a book. In this text, Picchi explains boats and sailing in an understandable, accessible way that will not intimidate a novice. An experienced anthropologist who has studied Brazilian and Mexican societies, she describes in vivid and colorful terms the many New England communities they visit.

Tom Desrosiers is a life-long resident of New Hampshire. He retired with the title Dean Emeritus from Academia. He has been sailing most of his adult life on lakes, coastal waters, and transatlantic and Caribbean adventures. The boats he has captained boats range from a twenty-five-foot Cape Dory sloop to a ten-meter yacht. His Pearson Triton Northstar (#516) was purchased on Long Island, sailed to Maine, destroyed in Hurricane Gloria and rebuilt by Tom and his wife Debra. His thirty-seven-foot Endeavour Makai was purchased in St. Thomas and sailed extensively in the Virgin Islands. He and Debra brought the boat to Maine in 1989 and have enjoyed many years of New England coastal sailing on this wonderful boat.

Printed in the United States
By Bookmasters